the golden guide to
scuba diving
by wheeler j. north

HANDBOOK
OF UNDERWATER
ACTIVITIES

A GOLDEN | HANDBOOK | GOLDEN PRESS, NEW YORK

contents

Assistance in the writing from my wife Barbara is gratefully acknowledged.

PHOTO CREDITS
Cover: Burton McNeely. AMF Voit: 35. Culver Pictures (from *Illustrated London News*, June 4, 1853): 7. Dolphin Products: 135 bottom right. Foul Anchor Archives: 123 right. French Embassy Press & Information Division: 126. Larry Jones: 68, 69. David Leighton: 101 top. Conrad Limbaugh: (courtesy Scripps Institution of Oceanography) 82; 92. Burton McNeely: 148. New York Zoological Society: 95 middle & bottom. Chuck Nicklin: 8, 9, 10, 20, 71, 72, 80, 90 left, 91 left, 93 bottom right, 98 top, 104 top, 108, 111, 113, 114, 117, 124, 128, 133, 135 top, 136 bottom left, 138 right, 139, 147 top. Wheeler North: 4, 11, 16, 18, 28, 31, 32, 33, 37, 39, 40, 41, 43 bottom left & right, 44, 46, 48, 49, 50, 51, 52, 54, 57, 58, 59, 61, 62, 63, 67, 74, 75, 76, 77, 79, 81, 85, 88, 90 right, 91 right, 93 top & bottom left, 96, 98 bottom, 101 bottom, 103, 104 bottom left & right, 110, 116, 118, 119, 122, 123 left, 125, 127, 132, 135 bottom left, 136 bottom right, 138 left, 140, 142, 144, 147 bottom. Pederson Brothers: 136 top. Seattle Public Aquarium: 95 top. Peter Throckmorton: 120. U.S. Navy: (by Dr. R. Dill) 43 top, 83; 150, 151, 152, 155, 157. U. of California, Scripps Institution of Oceanography: 154.

man in the underwater

1

The basic techniques and knowledge needed to enter our newest frontier—the exotic underwater world—are not difficult to acquire. The beginner, under the instruction of a skilled diver, learns how to move, breathe, and think underwater. He learns, too, that safety always comes first, since the underwater is a strange and often dangerous environment. And, as his diving proficiency increases, he works toward enlarging his knowledge and experience of the underwater world.

This book provides the fundamentals for being at home in all natural waters—oceans, rivers, lakes, bays, and estuaries. As different as these environments are from each other, the same principles of diving apply to all. A beginner should not go deeper than 30 feet; yet within this safety limit he can experience the full wonder and challenge of the underwater.

Marine research team
records animal specimens attached
to 30-year-old wreck
in waters off Pacific Coast.

HISTORY OF DIVING

Man's knowledge of the underwater world has been accumulated over many centuries. The need for food provided the earliest stimulus to dive, but military applications, salvage, and the quest for treasure have been important motives since Herodotus' time (460 B.C.).

The world beneath the surface differs from the world of dry land in three important ways. First: The viscosity of water makes movement slower and more laborious. Energy cannot be expended in the same way as on land, or even as in ordinary swimming. Second: Vision is reduced, and must be aided by other senses or techniques, most importantly navigational skill. Third: Great pressures occur underwater, requiring compensation if the body is to maintain its natural and efficient function.

Two of the simplest diving techniques, skin and Scuba diving (pronounced *skooba*), will be considered here. Skin diving is 30- to 60-second submergence during which the diver does not inhale. Scuba diving requires a "self-contained underwater breathing apparatus" that allows a diver to remain submerged for up to two hours.

Apparatus utilizing compressed air and hoses dates from the helmet invented by August Siebe in 1819. In 1825 an apparatus was invented that employed pure oxygen in closed-circuit systems (no liberation of bubbles), and was free of connections to the surface.

Open-circuit Scuba (bubbles exhaled into the water) dates back to 1925. Since then the system has been improved to the point where it is safe, simple, and cheap—a readily available tool for important and far-reaching underwater explorations. With it, almost anyone can dive and enjoy the pleasures and inspirations of the deep.

In 1853 a French inventor, M. Sicard, demonstrated a self-contained diving apparatus remarkably similar to modern Scuba.

ORIENTATION

This book is not intended to take the place of an instructor. It outlines the techniques that will qualify a diver for shallow diving, that is, to a depth of about 30 feet. Safe diving at deeper levels requires the same basic skills; but only after a diver has made these skills habitual and is at ease underwater can he cope with the problems encountered at greater depths: cold, increased hazard, decreased illumination, and deep-diving maladies. Anyone who is a fair swimmer can usually learn the basics of shallow-depth diving in a few hours. The learner who concentrates advances rapidly.

Disciplined alertness is as necessary for good diving as

physical prowess. For example: A diver who is underweighted and thereby tends to float can easily compensate by carrying stones; but unless he is alert, he may become too absorbed by his surroundings to be aware of the need for adjustment.

To be truly oriented in the underwater and to perceive its fascinations, the diver needs a basic knowledge of aquatic biology and submarine geology. With this knowledge he knows what to look for and how to interpret what he sees. For excitement and occasional rewards, the diver can follow specialized diving activities, such as spearfishing and underwater photography. Some divers, as discussed on pages 149 to 151, even earn their living underwater.

9

The underwater world
is alien to man; divers must
adapt to cold,
darkness, strange forms of life.

SAFETY

The need for safety in underwater activities can't be emphasized too much. Plenty of common sense, strict adherence to the rules, and a relaxed frame of mind form the ideal approach. Beginners should not be discouraged by the many things they have to keep in mind all at once, since the various safety procedures can be made habitual very quickly. The safe way is usually the easiest way. For example, holding the breath while ascending must be avoided in Scuba diving to prevent lung damage; but correct breathing will usually become natural to the diver after an hour or two of concentrated pool work, so that he will no longer need to keep this important rule foremost in mind.

Skilled swimmer (above) hitches
ride with saltwater sunfish, not a sport
for beginners. Opposite: Divers
carefully inspect wreck before entering.

JUDGMENT

A diver's judgment is his ability to think and make *wise* decisions while underwater. Even experienced divers sometimes do unwise things. At first it is difficult to think at all while underwater, and beginners often come to the surface to solve a bothersome problem, such as a loose mask strap. From the start, make a conscious effort to think through such minor troubles while submerged. Learn to anticipate them and to prevent their happening. Review each dive afterward and note how your decisions and actions might have been improved. Do not be ashamed of fear. The instinct that a novice shuns as cowardice is often respected as "cautious judgment" by old-timers. The other extreme, overconfidence, should also be avoided.

SENSE PERCEPTION

Sense perception is considerably altered in the underwater. Sound travels much faster and the direction of its source is difficult to detect. Time seems to pass very quickly, perhaps due to preoccupation with a strange environment. However, the changes most disorienting for the beginner are those in seeing and movement.

In the clearest water, maximum visibility is 200 feet; average distances are 10 to 50 feet. This condition has two causes: absorption and scattering. Water absorbs light much more readily than does air. If visibility is poor because water has absorbed most of the available daylight, flashlights or other artificial lighting will improve the situation. If light has been reduced by tiny particles suspended in the water (scattering), artificial lights will not help, since the suspended particles will reflect most of the light rays. Navigating under these conditions requires a compass and skill in interpreting environmental clues. Added difficulty comes from optical phenomena such as refraction (which is discussed on page 129).

Divers must also train themselves in the matter of energy output. The watery environment demands a continuous expenditure of energy for movement, maintenance of body temperature, and mental activity. Even resting on the bottom requires a moderate work output. Most novice divers fail to take this into account in planning their objectives. They attempt to do too much, ignore the signs of fatigue, and suddenly find themselves in a state of exhaustion, from which recovery is slow.

The rule is this: Maintain a reserve of strength. Pay close attention to the early symptoms of fatigue, and make it a habit to slow down before exhaustion leaves you no choice.

GAS SPACES OF THE BODY

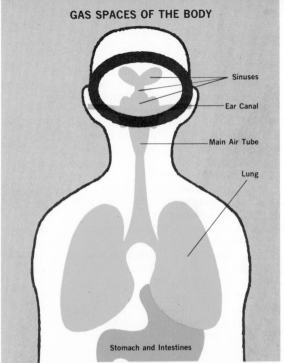

Sinuses

Ear Canal

Main Air Tube

Lung

Stomach and Intestines

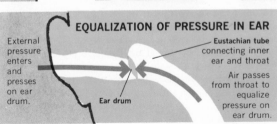

EQUALIZATION OF PRESSURE IN EAR

External pressure enters and presses on ear drum.

Ear drum

Eustachian tube connecting inner ear and throat

Air passes from throat to equalize pressure on ear drum.

EFFECTS OF PRESSURE

The well-being of divers in the underwater depends on how they respect two inexorable physical laws—Boyle's and Henry's—describing the behavior of gases under pressure.

The gases that concern a diver are the air he breathes and the nitrogen in his blood. The pressure on these gases (and on all underwater objects) is the weight of the earth's atmosphere plus that of the overlying water. At sea level, atmospheric pressure is 14.7 pounds per square inch (psi) or "one atmosphere." Underwater it is an additional 0.445 psi for each foot the diver descends. At 33 feet it is 29.4 psi, or 2 atmospheres.

Boyle's law states that if the pressure on a gas in a confined space is increased, the density of the gas increases in like manner, and its volume decreases proportionally. For instance, a quart of air at sea level is squeezed to half a quart at 33 feet underwater as the pressure mounts from 1 atmosphere to 2. This also has the effect of doubling the density of the air molecules. (Liquids and solids—unlike gases—compress negligibly at the pressures encountered in diving.)

Squeezes: Air in a diver's sinuses and ear passages is "gas in a confined space." Under the increasing pressure of a descent these spaces cannot lessen volume as required by Boyle's law because they are enclosed by rigid bone. They are connected to larger air passages by small openings. If these openings are clogged by mucus, the transfer of air into the sinuses and ear passages—necessary to build up counterpressures—is interfered with. The result is a "squeeze," a painful stress on the tissue linings and membranes. Unless it is relieved, ruptures and other serious physical damage may result.

14

BOYLE'S LAW

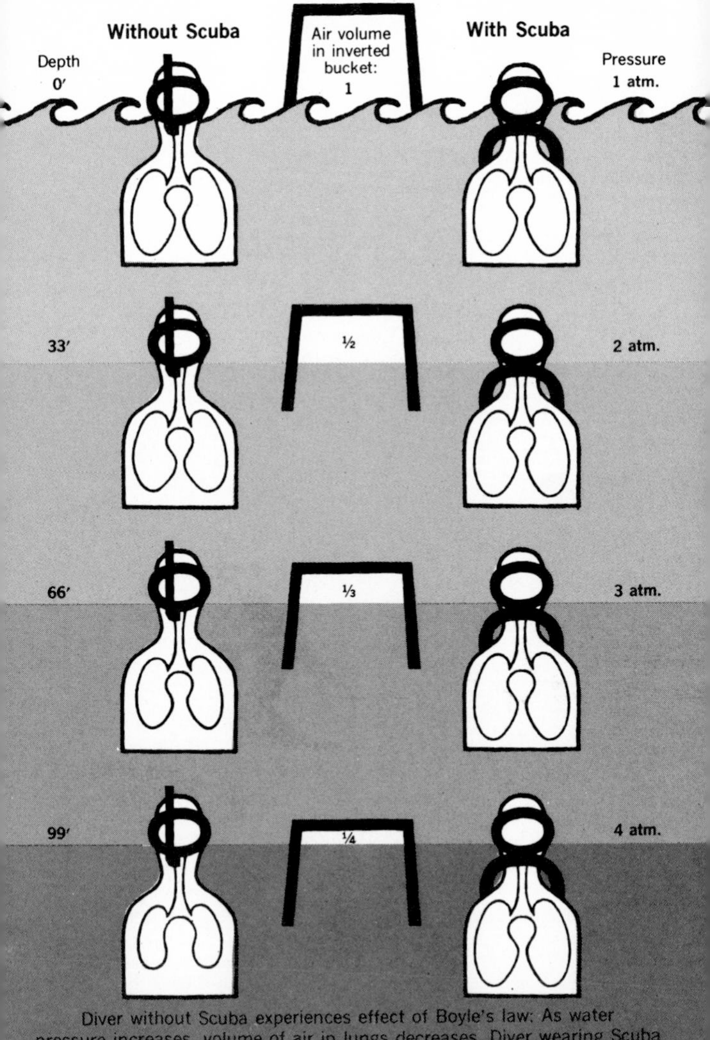

Without Scuba

Depth

0'

33'

66'

99'

Air volume in inverted bucket:

1

½

⅓

¼

With Scuba

Pressure

1 atm.

2 atm.

3 atm.

4 atm.

Diver without Scuba experiences effect of Boyle's law: As water pressure increases, volume of air in lungs decreases. Diver wearing Scuba has an air supply that keeps air volume in lungs constant.

Squeezes are cleared by equalizing internal and external pressures. In most cases this can be done by opening and closing the jaws, yawning, or swallowing. An obstinate squeeze may call for removing the face mask, holding the nose closed with the fingers, and snorting forcefully. The

To clear obstinate ear or sinus squeeze, diver removes face mask, holds nose closed, snorts forcefully. Pressure stretches clogged ear passages.

pressure of blowing helps to stretch clogged passages, thereby allowing internal counterpressures to enter the spaces containing low-pressure gas.

Squeezes can also occur inside a face mask—another "confined space." If allowed to continue, squeezes can rupture capillaries and cause bloodshot eyes, but they are easily counteracted by blowing more air into the mask through the nose.

The lungs are never squeezed because they are flexible and not rigidly enclosed. The Scuba regulator delivers air at the pressure of the surrounding water level. However, according to Boyle's formula, the density of the air molecules increases with increasing pressure, and the deeper a diver goes, the more molecules are inhaled and exhaled with each breath. Therefore, at a constant rate of breathing, a diver's tank of air will last only half as long at 99 feet (4 atmospheres) as at 33 feet (2 atmospheres).

Ascent: The reverse of Boyle's law also applies. A decrease in pressure likewise decreases density, but increases volume proportionally. This is of profound importance to an ascending diver, for as water pressure decreases, air expanding in the "confined spaces" of the body presses against eardrums, sinus linings, etc., seeking release. These "reverse squeezes" are as painful as those encountered on descent. Those developing in the ears cause dizziness.

Clearing reverse squeezes requires pinching the nose and sucking hard to create a strong internal vacuum, again stretching the clogged passages. If a squeeze is allowed to continue, blood may be forced from the linings of the cavities into the face mask. Soreness may persist for a few hours after the dive, but need not cause concern unless discomfort increases or lasts several days.

Air Embolism: The most serious threat to the ascending diver is also the most easily avoided. This is the air embolism, a bubble traveling through the bloodstream, eventually blocking circulation and possibly causing extensive damage to organs thus cut off from a normal blood supply. If the brain or nerves are involved, pain and paralysis may occur.

Air embolism is a direct result of holding the breath during ascent. Unless a diver exhales normally, the rapid

AIR EMBOLISM

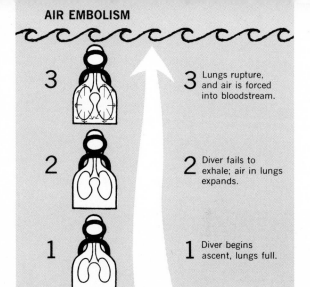

3 — Lungs rupture, and air is forced into bloodstream.

2 — Diver fails to exhale; air in lungs expands.

1 — Diver begins ascent, lungs full.

expansion of air may rupture the air sacs and blood vessels of his lungs. Bubbles of high-pressure air are forced into the bloodstream and become dangerous embolisms.

Air embolism occurs infrequently, but it can strike in as little as 8 feet of water and must be guarded against by all divers. The simple and complete protection against it is to breathe normally on ascent.

GAS ABSORPTION

Henry's law says that the amount of gas which dissolves in a liquid is proportional to the partial pressure that it exerts. This means that as a diver descends, and as the pressure upon him increases, gas is more readily absorbed into his bloodstream and tissues. At 2 atmospheres, al-

To clear reverse squeeze,
sometimes encountered while ascending,
pinch nose and suck hard
to create strong internal vacuum.

most twice as much gas can be absorbed by the blood as at 1 atmosphere. Conversely, decreasing the partial pressure of a gas absorbed in a liquid by one half will liberate one half the gas from solution.

Inhaled air is roughly 78 percent nitrogen and 21 percent oxygen, with a trace of other gases, chiefly carbon dioxide. Oxygen dissolved in the bloodstream is utilized in metabolism; carbon dioxide is exhaled as a waste product. Nitrogen is inert and is neither used nor produced. Under the terms of Henry's law, however, increasing underwater pressure increases the amount of nitrogen absorbed in the blood. This is not a serious factor in dives of 30 feet or less. As a diver ascends, normal respiration helps eliminate the nitrogen that has been absorbed into the blood. Surfacing from deeper dives must be more gradual due to greater nitrogen absorption.

Anoxia: Divers who hold their breath too long risk losing consciousness due to lack of oxygen (O_2). This can happen even on brief, shallow dives. Oxygen deficiency of itself does not cause the distress associated with anoxia; this results from an excessive amount of carbon dioxide (CO_2), normally eliminated by regular breathing. To prevent anoxia, limit breath-holding to one minute at the most, and take care to fill tanks with clean, filtered air.

It is a practice of many skin divers to "hyperventilate," or prebreathe, before descending. They take nine or ten rapid, deep breaths, thereby building up O_2 and removing CO_2. This enables them to reach deeper levels and to stay submerged longer, but the practice has its risks. Occasionally on ascending, these divers lose consciousness, presumably succumbing to anoxia when oxygen pressure drops during the ascent.

21

Ascending divers pause
for decompression stop. Fixed schedule
must be followed when
ascending from lengthy, deep dives.

Nausea: This can strike a diver without warning from such causes as reverse ear squeeze, too rapid descent, motion sickness due to wave surge, or prolonged fatigue. Its symptoms are felt as acutely underwater as on the surface. Vomiting may occur, necessitating removal of the mouthpiece. After the spasm has passed, the diver must be careful not to gasp for air before he has replaced the mouthpiece. Never dive if you feel seasick while still on the surface.

Respiratory Fatigue: Fatigued chest muscles make breathing arduous. A poorly adjusted regulator can cause this, as well as over-exertion. If it should happen before your work underwater is completed, rest awhile, then pace your output carefully.

Carbon Dioxide Poisoning: An excess of this normal waste product can result from poor equipment (a hard-breathing regulator), bad air, or prolonged breath-holding. A feeling of exhaustion appears, although little work may have been done; headache and nausea follow in severe cases. Rest and fresh air are the remedies.

Carbon Monoxide Poisoning: Beware of carbon monoxide. It can enter a Scuba tank if the compressor used to fill the tank is powered by a gasoline engine positioned so that the air intake is downwind from the exhaust. It can also be produced as a breakdown product when a compressor that has been lubricated with oil is allowed to overheat.

CO poisoning causes extreme weakness leading to unconsciousness. The victim shows a reddish, flushed face and cherry-colored lips. In very severe cases breathing may stop, requiring artificial respiration. Mild cases will respond to rest and fresh air. To prevent CO poisoning, carefully follow tank-filling procedures on page 35.

Uglies: This disorder, of unknown cause, involves dizziness, faintness, or a narrowing of the field of vision at the end of a rapid, deep descent. The condition lasts a few minutes at most, after which activities can be resumed.

MALADIES OF DEEP DIVING

Divers who may be tempted to go below the 30- to 40-foot level should know something about the disorders that can occur in deep diving.

Nitrogen Narcosis: Under high pressure, the nitrogen in a diver's air supply can dull his senses, impairing alertness and efficiency. He may lose his sense of direction and in a state of intoxication descend to more dangerous levels. Cold and increased depth tend to worsen the effect. The danger zone for most compressed-air divers begins at about 100 feet, although the effect has been known to occur at shallower levels. A diver who feels the "rapture of the deep" coming on should ascend to a safe level and remain there until he returns to normal.

Bends (decompression sickness, caisson disease): Ascending from a lengthy dive at levels deeper than 30 feet reduces pressure and causes the blood to release gas it has been holding in solution. If ascent is too rapid, bubbles of nitrogen form in the diver's tissues and bloodstream (similar to the bubbling of a carbonated beverage when uncapped). Extreme pain and paralysis result.

Prevention of this condition requires gradual decrease of pressure according to a fixed schedule (U.S. Navy Decompression Tables, pages 24–25). However, as long as a diver goes no deeper than 30 feet, he can stay underwater indefinitely without requiring decompression on his ascent to the surface.

On his shallow dives, the beginner will not have to refer to decompression tables. They are shown here (for depths to 130 feet) to illustrate the relationship between time spent at particular depths and time required on ascent for safe release of nitrogen from the blood. They are based on a rate of ascent of 60 feet per minute.

United States Navy Decompression Tables (abridged)							
Depth of dive (feet)	Time on bottom (minutes)	Stops (feet and minutes)				Sum of times at various stops (minutes)	Approximate total decompression time (minutes)
		Feet 40	Feet 30	Feet 20	Feet 10		
40	200				0	0	1
40	230				7	7	8
40	250				11	11	12
40	270				15	15	16
50	100				0	0	1
50	120				5	5	6
50	160				21	21	22
50	220				40	40	41
60	60				0	0	1
60	80				7	7	8
60	120				26	26	27
60	160				48	48	49
60	180				56	56	57
60	200				69	70	71
70	50				0	0	1
70	70				14	14	15
70	100				33	33	34
70	120				47	51	52
70	140			4	56	64	65
70	160			8	72	85	86

Depth of dive (feet)	Time on bottom (minutes)	Stops (feet and minutes)				Sum of times at various stops (minutes)	Approximate total decompression time (minutes)
		Feet 40	Feet 30	Feet 20	Feet 10		
80	40				0	0	2
80	60				17	17	18
80	80			2	31	33	34
80	110			13	53	66	67
80	130			19	63	82	83
80	150			32	77	109	110
90	30				0	0	2
90	50				18	18	20
90	70			7	30	37	38
90	90			18	48	66	67
90	110			24	61	85	86
90	130		5	36	74	115	116
100	25				0	0	2
100	30				3	3	5
100	50			2	24	26	28
100	70			17	39	56	58
100	90		3	23	57	83	84
100	110		10	34	72	116	117
100	120		12	41	78	131	132
110	20				0	0	2
110	30				7	7	9
110	50			8	26	34	36
110	70		1	23	48	72	74
110	90		12	30	64	106	108
120	15				0	0	2
120	30				14	14	16
120	50			15	31	46	48
120	70		9	23	55	87	89
120	90		19	37	74	130	132
130	10				0	0	2
130	20				4	4	6
130	40			10	25	35	37
130	70		16	24	61	101	103
130	90	8	19	45	80	152	154

PHYSICAL FITNESS

Good health is necessary for diving and, if frequent and continual activity is contemplated, it is wise to be examined every year by a physician. The following list details the items of particular importance for a diving medical examination.

Ears: no tympanic perforation.
Nose, Sinuses, and Throat: free from chronic infections, canals and passages unobstructed.
Eyes: free from chronic disorders.
Limbs: no serious disabilities.
Heart, Lungs: no defects.
Psychiatric: emotional stability.
General: correct weight, good coordination.
Laboratory: chest X ray.

If you have just recovered from a long or serious illness, have a thorough medical examination before diving again.

Do *Not* Dive if you are:
obese ■ unduly sensitive to cold

Susceptible to:
nausea ■ motion sickness
claustrophobia

Or if you have:
a heart condition ■ chronic chest disease
disorders of the middle ear

WARNING

1 The underwater is an alien environment. Respect it!

2 Always dive with a partner, **never** alone.

3 Dive only when in top physical condition. Do not dive with a cold (pressure cannot be equalized when sinuses are clogged), when tired, or after taking medicinal drugs or alcohol.

4 Check all equipment in shallow water to be sure it is functioning properly.

5 Stay alert. Keep calm. Don't panic. Most underwater accidents are the result of human carelessness rather than equipment failure.

6 Never ascend faster than 60 feet per minute on ordinary dives. (In an emergency, as fast as 300 feet per minute is tolerable.)

7 Know the *Red Cross Lifesaving Manual* procedures, particularly artificial respiration techniques. If an accident occurs, start artificial respiration immediately, even in the water while towing the victim. Subsequently, give the attending physician all details of what occurred.

equipment

Keep your equipment simple. Underwater movement is awkward even with minimum gear, so make each item contribute positively to the dive at hand. Following are the qualities to look for when you buy basic skin and Scuba diving equipment.

Face Mask: The rubber should be soft enough to fit the contours of the face and achieve a watertight seal. (Test by pressing mask against face without using headstrap. Inhale gently; the air vacuum should hold the mask in place.) The lens should be clear, untinted, shatterproof glass. (Plastic scratches and fogs.) Some masks have built-in holders for eyeglasses. Lenses can also be prescription-ground. For nearsighted divers the faceplate acts as a lens underwater. Do not use goggles; external pressures cannot be equalized as they can in a face mask and eye injury may result.

A wise diver travels
light, chooses equipment that
fits well, operates simply,
and gives maximum performance.

Exposure Suits: In water below 64 degrees F. protective clothing is necessary to hold body heat at a normal level. For the average diver, the "wet suit" of neoprene foam rubber is best. Insulation is provided by the thousands of air bubbles imprisoned in the foam; no underwear is required. The small amount of water that normally leaks into the suit (hence its name) is quickly warmed to body temperature and does not lessen the suit's effectiveness. Suits range from 1/8- to 1/4-inch thick. The amount of insulation required depends on diving conditions and the diver's cold tolerance. A 3/16-inch suit usually is adequate for temperatures as low as 55 degrees F.

A ready-made wet suit costs about $30 to $55, a custom suit $60. Choose black rather than a bright color which may attract dangerous fish.

The so-called "dry suit," tightly sealed at wrists, ankles, face, and neck to keep water out, is preferred by professionals who must work in extremely cold water or remain below for long periods of time. It is usually made of thin rubber sheeting and worn over one or two suits of thermal underwear, or even over a wet suit.

There are dry suits designed to be entered from the front, the back, or the waist; the front-entry type is usually easiest to get on and off. Cost of a dry suit, including material and labor, is about $100.

The main disadvantage of the dry suit is that the thin rubber sheeting is susceptible to leaks and tears—and the suit is ineffective once water has entered it.

Fins: Proper fit is essential. Fins are the principal means of locomotion underwater (they triple the power of your kick) and should be neither so loose as to slip off nor so tight as to cause chafing, cramped muscles, or cold feet.

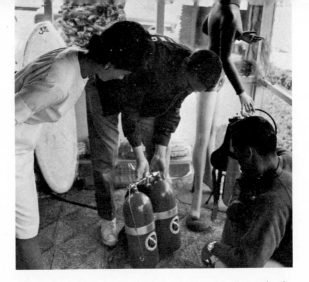

Special triangular rubber bands are available that grip the heel of a loose-fitting fin. You can buy either floating or sinking fins; the floating type is generally best for the average diver.

Snorkel: This tube, with mouthpiece, is used for breathing surface air. The ideal type is J-shaped, 15 to 20 inches long, with comfortable mouthpiece. Avoid float valves designed to close when the entire tube is submerged. They don't work very well. When swimming on the surface, Scuba divers use the snorkel to save tank air.

Weightbelt: This must have a foolproof safety buckle that can be released instantly underwater with one hand. See that the web strap is adjustable; the belt goes on last and must circle your gear as well as you, so as to fall freely if jettisoned in an emergency. The belt should thread easily through the lead weights.

31

Experienced divers usually
use two-tank gear, but equipment
should be selected
to meet individual needs.

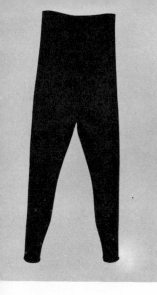

Maintenance: With normal care, your exposure suit will last for years. Sprinkle powder liberally inside the suit and on yourself to reduce friction when pulling the suit on. Ordinary talcs won't do for this, as they contain oil which deteriorates rubber. You can buy the right kind of powder at your skin-diving supply store.

After a saltwater dive, rinse your suit in fresh water. For storing, clean and powder your suit and hang it in a cool, dry place, making sure that the surfaces are not stuck together at any point. Never fold the suit.

Glue, cleaning fluid, and patching material are available at most diving stores. To make a repair, clean rubber thoroughly, apply glue, let dry till tacky, then press pieces or edges firmly together. If possible, press between boards until dry (½ hour).

Wet suit consists of pants, shirt, hood. Fins give stability, propulsion. Weightbelt has quick-release hitch; lower mask has snorkel attached.

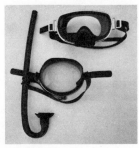

What to Wear Underwater	
Water Temperature	**Equipment**
Above 75° F.	Ordinary bathing suit
65°–70°	Rubber shirt and hood ⎫
50°–65°	Add rubber trousers ⎬ Wet suit
Below 50°	Add boots and mittens ⎭
40°	Dry suit & thermal underwear

Typical Weight Requirements (in pounds of lead)	
Dress	**Weight* to Add** (at 30 ft)
Bathing suit	0–8
⅛″ shirt & hood	4–12
⅛″ full suit	7–15
¼″ full suit	15–20
	*2–4 pounds less for deeper dives

Scuba: This apparatus enables a diver to operate independent of the surface by providing a portable air supply and a means of adjusting its pressure to that of the surrounding water. Scuba has three main parts: a steel tank containing filtered, compressed air; a regulator which reduces the pressure of tank air to that of the diver's water level, and which releases air only "on demand" (as diver inhales); a hose which connects mouthpiece and regulator.

Most Scuba systems are open circuit; air is exhaled through a one-way valve in the regulator and escapes in a stream of bubbles. (Professional divers may use a closed circuit, or rebreather, system. The carbon dioxide is filtered out of exhaled air and oxygen is returned to be rebreathed. Much more tank air is actually used, therefore, than in the simpler but more wasteful open-circuit systems.)

The standard tank contains 70 cubic feet of air (usually at about 2,000 pounds psi; rated pressure is stamped on the tanks near the valve). This supply should last about an hour at a 30-foot depth. Tanks can be fitted with valves that warn the diver when his air is running low. The *automatic reserve* valve lessens the air flow as the supply dwindles. When the diver finds breathing becoming difficult, it is time to surface. The *constant reserve* valve closes when tank pressure drops to 300 psi and must be reopened manually to restore air flow. The diver knows he has a five-minute air reserve (at 30 feet; less lower down). Novice divers should breathe their unit empty under safe conditions to learn how it behaves. Air compressors used to fill the tank should not change the oxygen content of the air, or introduce CO_2, CO, oil, or water vapor. Filters are always necessary. The compressor should be run cool and free from exhaust fumes.

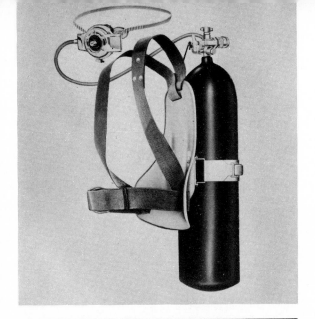

Tank-filling Techniques

Proceed slowly when filling a tank and if possible immerse it in cold water. The cooling allows it to be filled to a higher pressure, and is a practice that prolongs the working life of the tank.

Fill tanks only with air certified for breathing purposes *(Skin Diver* magazine lists all the approved refilling stations in the U.S.). Improperly compressed air may be low in oxygen or high in carbon dioxide, carbon monoxide, oil, and water vapors.

Do not refill conventional tanks with pure oxygen. Use of 100 percent oxygen in diving can be dangerous and requires special techniques.

Don't fill your tank beyond the rated pressure.

35

Self-contained underwater breathing apparatus, or Scuba, comprises tank containing compressed air, regulator, hose, and harness.

Maintenance: Keep equipment clean and maintained properly. Gear malfunction as a result of carelessness can cause diver fatigue and dangerous situations. However, *do not oil Scuba gear.* Oil and oxygen will explode if combined in pressurized air.

Never leave the regulator attached to the air tank when not in use. Rinse all openings except high-pressure valve with fresh water after each use. Place a stopper on high-pressure valve seat and hang the unit up to dry.

Tanks must be pressure-tested every five years. Dates of previous tests are stamped on the tank. Be sure your tank isn't out-of-date.

Handle charged air tanks gently. Be particularly careful about damage to valve. Never use regulator as a handhold when lifting tank.

Regulators: These supply compressed air to the diver in the amounts that he needs or demands. A two-stage regulator conducts high-pressure air from the tank to a chamber where pressure is reduced to about 100 psi, then to a second chamber where it is reduced to proper pressure for breathing. A single-stage regulator has only one chamber for reducing air pressure. The regulator automatically supplies air at a pressure that compensates for the pressure of the surrounding water.

At shallow depths (less than 30 feet), differences between single- and two-stage regulators are negligible. For deep diving, two-stage is preferable.

All single-hose units are two-stage regulators; double-hose units may be two-stage or single-stage. They perform equally well, though single-hose units may be easier to maintain. Your regulator should be overhauled by an expert at least once a year.

Diver tests regulator for comfort
and easy breathing. It regulates pressure
of tank air and supplies
air on demand as diver inhales.

Standards for Regulators

A good regulator should:

Be easy to purge when flooded—either by exhaling or by push-button action.

Be comfortable. It should have ample hose to allow full movement. Mouthpiece should not chafe gums or lips, should have a good biting surface for a secure grasp.

Breathe easily.

Provide a warning well before air runs out (if tank valve does not).

Be rugged, corrosion-proof, and streamlined to avoid snagging.

Be easy to maintain.

Underwater Lights: Battery-powered, waterproof lights may be purchased at most dive shops or can be easily improvised. An ordinary glass container with a rubber gasket seal will house a flashlight securely down to 15 to 20 feet. The light must be turned on beforehand, of course. Even simpler is the use of three or four plastic bags, one inside the other, tied off with knots or rubber bands. The innermost bag contains the flashlight and a sponge to take up any water seepage.

Compass: Many inexpensive waterproof compasses are now available. An instrument which can be strapped to the wrist is usually adequate for most navigation tasks. Be sure the markings are easily discernible in dim light (luminescent markings work well). It is usually not possible to navigate with extreme precision underwater, so a dial divided into single degrees may be more of a hindrance. Markings every 15 to 30 degrees and an arrow clearly defining North are sufficient.

Knife: Whether to carry a knife is a matter of individual preference. It is wise to have a knife when working around rope, lines, kelp, or other entangling objects. Knives may also be useful for digging or scraping when collecting specimens. They are almost never required for protection from animals because unprovoked attacks are extremely rare. The blade should be non-rusting stainless steel with a smooth cutting edge and a toothed edge for sawing. You can get either a floating or sinking knife; usually the sinking type is better since it can be laid down while working. A scabbard is a necessity. It either slips onto the weight belt or straps to a leg or arm. The latter variety will not be lost if you jettison the weightbelt. Underwater, as anywhere else, a sharp knife is safer than a dull knife.

Accessories (from top):
Waterproof light, knife and scabbard,
combination depth gauge and
compass with luminescent markings.

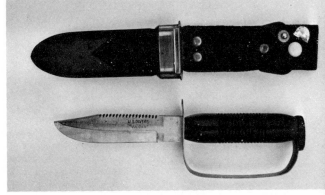

Tools: Almost any tool which is used on dry land functions well underwater. To prevent loss, it is usually best to attach a line and loop the other end around your wrist or belt, especially when working on the underside of a boat in deep water or over a turbid bottom. Rinse a tool in fresh water after use, then dry and oil it to prevent rusting.

Watch: Underwater watches are convenient but expensive and are usually not necessary for shallow-water work. (They are essential, however, on deep dives for regulating decompression times.) Rubber or nylon straps are better than ordinary cloth, leather, or metal. Once you learn the approximate length of time a tank of air will last, a watch can be used as an approximate indicator of the underwater time you have remaining.

Have flotation gear as stand-by
emergency equipment. Diver above has raft,
lady diver has instantly inflatable
Mae West, plus easily jettisoned weightbelt.

Flotation Devices: Always have a device you can use to help you stay afloat when you want to. The standard life jacket (Mae West) can be blown up by mouth (often difficult in an emergency) or instantly inflated with a CO_2 cartridge. (Do not depend on a cartridge that is more than three months old, as they deteriorate.) The Res-Q-Pak, a rubber belt with water wings folded into a small packet, is also cartridge-inflated. The used Mae West inflating cartridge can be replaced; the Res-Q-Pak is good for one use only. A foam-rubber suit is excellent flotation after you jettison your weightbelt. Anchored boats, rubber rafts, or inner tubes are suitable too. If you travel far underwater, your raft or tube must be towed along; if you have a boat, a companion can guide it by following your air bubbles. 41

First-aid Kit: Minor cuts and punctures occur frequently in diving, so keep a first-aid kit handy. Contents should include bandages, adhesive tape, an antiseptic, small scissors, tweezers, ammonia (for jellyfish and hydroid stings), and seasickness pills.

Diving Flag: For both skin and Scuba diving, display a standard diving flag from your boat, raft, etc. Other boats will stay clear and will not mistake your equipment as abandoned.

Depth Gauge: Depths less than 20 feet are easily estimated by glancing up at the surface. But if you are deeper or water is murky, a gauge will tell you how deep you are, and give accurate positions for collecting or photographing. The gauge is essential for measuring decompression stops.

Pressure Gauge: One type, for topside use only, is handy to measure unused air in your tank after a short dive. Enough for the next task? Also useful is the Seevue gauge, which monitors pressure underwater, enabling you to judge time remaining during the dive.

Equipment for Special Uses: The Hookah rig is a small compressor with a regulator and long hose. Set up in a boat or on the beach, it provides cheap diving for long periods, although mobility is restricted by the hose.

Oxygen rebreathers (so-called closed-circuit apparatus) are used for work where absence of bubbles is desirable, as in photography of timid fish. Since the gas is reused, there is no telltale trail of bubbles. Inherent hazards restrict rebreathers for use only by trained experts.

Full canvas suit and helmet (hard hat) permit long and strenuous work at great depths. Expense of equipment, training, and operation limits their use largely to commercial work.

42

For longer submergence, diver (top) wears double tank. Oxygen rebreathing apparatus (right) prevents formation of bubbles. Boat (far right) flies diving flag.

training

3

Time now for the first dive. This is best done in the clear, quiet water of a swimming pool, under the eye of a competent instructor. Here the diver can subject himself to such commonplace problems as a flooded face mask or an empty air tank with no anxiety about being in real trouble. Only in this way can he gain the physical and psychological experience he must have before entering natural underwater environments.

In putting on diving equipment, follow this sequence: exposure suit, air tank and regulator, weightbelt, accessories (knife, watch, etc.), mask, and fins. Partners can help each other with the cumbersome tanks.

Check Scuba before entering water by taking two or three breaths. If it is functioning properly, enter pool to waist depth and put on fins. Recheck gear by submersion. Adjust anything that is leaky or loose.

Beginner in pool practices
ditching equipment. Four or five
hours of pool instruction
should precede natural-water dives.

Neutral Buoyancy: This is the ideal point of balance at which the diver neither sinks nor rises. It is difficult to maintain; an air tank may lighten as much as ten pounds as it empties, exposure suits lose buoyancy by compression as the diver descends, and there may be several pounds' difference between inhalation and exhalation. Still, an approximation of neutral buoyancy can be achieved by adding or subtracting belt weights. During pool training, practice diving when too light, too heavy, and at neutral buoyancy.

Clearing the Snorkel: Water can be forced from the snorkel by a short, vigorous exhalation. Then inhale gently to test for residual water. If tube is not clear, make sure it is vertical and repeat procedure.

Clearing the Mask: Accept the fact that most masks leak a little. Realize, too, that some water sloshing in the mask helps clear the faceplate of fog. A flooded mask, however, must be emptied and the technique is simple. Tilt the head up. Press mask against the forehead to tighten the seal. Blow hard through the nose. The air will force the water out at the lower edge of the mask, across the wearer's upper lip.

Once this is mastered, practice removing the mask completely, replacing it, and clearing. Pretend your mask strap has broken and practice swimming while holding the mask to your face with one hand. Throw your mask some distance away and practice search and recovery. Put it on and clear. Trade masks with other divers and learn to clear different types.

Clearing Mouthpiece and Hose: Everyone gets water in his breathing hose once in a while. The easiest way to dispose of a slight seepage is to swallow it. More water than this

can be expelled in one of several ways. A single-hose regulator can be cleared by exhaling gently through the mouthpiece, or by pressing the purging button. Practice purging with mouthpiece in and out.

For a flooded double-hose regulator, roll to left (side on which exhaust tube is located) and exhale vigorously two or three times. Air will force water out of exhaust vent. To clear intake tube, raise mouthpiece above head (higher than regulator) and let escaping air blow water out.

47

Water often must be expelled
from breathing hose. Diver above clears
intake tube on double-hose
regulator by raising mouthpiece.

Swimming with Scuba: Swim back and forth several times in shallow water before proceeding to the deep end of the pool. Use a flutter kick, bending your knees slightly. Arms contribute little compared to your fins and are best held loosely to your sides for better streamlining. Guard against squeezes as you descend and breathe normally to prevent air embolism when you rise. Repeat all of your shallow-end work at the deep end, including mask and hose clearing, and practice turning your air off and on. When you feel at home, practice pulling off masks unexpectedly with your partner and shutting off each other's air; this develops quick responses and self-confidence.

The novice should not be disappointed if he cannot descend more than a few feet on his first dives. For some

Above: Scuba beginner practices
turning air on and off. Opposite: Divers
share air as "donor"
passes mouthpiece to "leech."

people several weeks of diving practice is necessary before the Eustachian tubes of the inner ears accustom themselves to rapid changes in pressure and diving becomes comfortable.

Sharing Air: This is a useful technique to know in case of equipment malfunction. Learn it both as "donor" and as "leech," and with both single- and double-hose regulators. Take a full breath and hand your mouthpiece to the leech, who quickly draws two or three breaths and returns it. Clear it, take two or three breaths, and repeat the procedure. With a double-hose regulator, the leech must be several inches above the donor. Practice while motionless, swimming horizontally, and ascending. Hold onto each other's harness when moving.

49

On the Surface: While resting or swimming on the surface switch to snorkel breathing to conserve tank air.

Water Entries: Try standing, kneeling, sitting, and back entries at the deep end—with mouthpiece in and out; mask on and off; air on and off. Protect the face-mask lens with your hand and draw your head in toward your shoulders to prevent neck strain.

Ditch and Recovery: To escape from an underwater entanglement, it may be necessary to remove equipment. Practice this. Pass the tank over the head or around the shoulder. Placing the weightbelt over it to hold it down, turn air off, jettison fins and mask, and ascend slowly, exhaling vigorously.

To recover, descend again to the bottom and drape weightbelt over one arm to keep you there; replace mouthpiece and turn on air; begin breathing. Now lay the weightbelt

From left: Divers practice
forward and backward entries,
tank removal, and
overhead recovery of tank.

across your lap or knee (put weightbelt on if tank harness
has no crotch strap), put on the tank, followed by weightbelt, mask, and finally fins.

Exhaustion of Air: Most Scuba systems provide warning
before the tank air is exhausted. Breathe your gear "dry"
to learn its behavior. Note any differences in the air supply
in shallow and in deep water, and observe the duration of
the reserve supply, if provided. A two-hose regulator will
deliver the last of the air if you roll over on your back.

End of Session: Shut off your air supply and swim 200 feet
wearing or towing your gear. This simulates the swim back
to shore. Swimming on your back utilizes the buoyancy of
the empty tank. Leave the pool carefully and dismantle
gear immediately.

The average person should have four or five hours of
pool training before diving in natural water.

51

first dives

With a partner, you are now ready to try your pool-learned techniques in natural water environments. Make first dives in favorable weather and select a diving area that is shallow, clear, and calm. Expect a slight increase of buoyancy in salt water. In freshwater places you may have to take into account seasonal temperature changes, murkiness, pollution, and strong currents. Always study an environment carefully for several minutes before you enter it, particularly for changing wave and tide conditions.

Make every dive a planned operation. You and your partner should agree on the purpose of the dive (training, recreation, collecting, etc.), location or destination, expected duration, probable depths, regular and special equipment. Use good judgment in deciding how much to attempt. Anticipate problems and be ready to alter objectives or adjust gear as required—even during the dive.

First dives should be made
in diving area that is shallow and
calm, under supervision of
partner or—preferably—instructor.

Waves within storm area are called
"sea" (top). Moving from storm center they
become uniform (middle), are called
"swell." They break on shore as "surf."

READING THE SURFACE

The study you make of the surface before submerging in a lake, river, or ocean will tell you much that can increase the safety and enjoyment of the dive. Here are some things to look for.

Waves: Large, storm-generated waves can travel hundreds or thousands of miles. The depth and force of the "wave surge"—the back-and-forth water movement as the waves pass overhead—is in proportion to the height of the waves and the length of time required for two crests to pass. Within a stormy area, the waves will be irregular in appearance and are called "sea." As they travel away, they become more uniform and evenly spaced and are called "swell." On reaching shallow water wave crests peak, then tumble or break over the advancing edge as "surf."

Frequently, waves from two widely separated storm centers will converge on the same coast. When crests from the two wave trains coincide (reinforcement), very large waves result. If a crest and a trough coincide (cancellation), a calmer sea is produced. Usually the wave trains are not exactly in phase and alternate periods of reinforcement and cancellation occur, separated in time by a few minutes. This is one reason why your study of the surface must not be hasty.

Surface Patterns: Bottom topography and other surface conditions can often be predicted from wave patterns on the surface. Waves travel faster in deep water; hence, although a straight coast with an evenly sloping bottom may be approached by waves at an oblique angle, the first portion of the wave to enter shallow water slows down and the entire wave eventually turns and approaches shore parallel to it.

WAVE PATTERNS
EVEN-SLOPING STRAIGHT SHELF

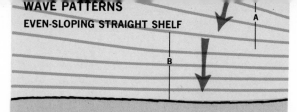

Waves approach straight coast obliquely. Wave-ends entering shallow water slow down (A), waves wheel and meet coast in straight formation (B).

SUBMARINE CANYON

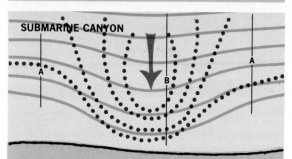

A submarine canyon will cause waves to converge on either side of it (A). The convergence areas display huge surf, while over canyon (B) waves diverge and are small.

SYMMETRICAL COVE

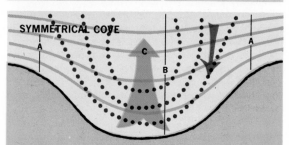

Small bay or cove that is deep in center will cause waves to converge on seaward edges (A) and break in heavy surf; in central area (B) waves will tend to diverge and break in gentle surf. Seaward riptide may be formed (C).

INTERACTION OF WAVE TRAINS FROM DIFFERENT DIRECTIONS

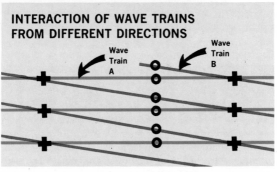

Wave Train A

Wave Train B

✚ = Reinforcement: crests coincide with crests

Train A

Train B

⭕ = Cancellation: crests coincide with troughs

Train A

Train B

Breaking wave (photo, top) reveals shallow spot. Divers alert to surface wave patterns can often predict bottom topography.

Currents: These water movements result from wind, waves, tides, gravity, and other forces. They are recognized by the flow of water they produce in the surrounding environment, by the movement of objects floating in them, or by streaks of discolored water or foam. Swift currents must be avoided. A conditioned swimmer in full Scuba can maintain a speed of only about one mph without tiring, so that a diver is in trouble if he must battle an appreciably faster current for any length of time. Frictional drag may reduce a current near the bottom, however, so that a diver can pull himself along the bottom against a current in which swimming would be futile. In a strong current, anchor your boat downstream from where you want to work and swim to the location along the bottom. When you are out of air you will be conveniently upstream from your boat.

Interrupted wave train,
discolored offshore water, and seaward
flow of foam are signs of
riptide (arrows in pictures above).

Expect rapid currents in the narrows of streams and rivers, alongside jetties, and at the entrances to bays, harbors, and estuaries when the tide is changing. Do not fight strong currents. Swim across or with them to the nearest land, or toward a calmer area.

Waves create currents in the direction of travel. When waves hit a beach obliquely, a "long-shore current" running parallel to the shore may appear.

Rip currents are localized "rivers" flowing seaward, returning water brought toward shore by the waves. Swimmers caught in rips should swim parallel to the shore until they are out of the current. Good swimmers, however, can use rips by riding them out to diving spots. You can recognize rips by their tendency to reduce the surf locally, and by their swift, seaward flow carrying discolored water and foam.

Diving from Shore: When entering through strong surf, put on your fins in shallow water and then walk backwards, otherwise the waves will topple you. When you are returning to shore through surf, remove your fins in waist-deep water, also to prevent toppling. If waves are breaking in water deeper than 4 or 5 feet, it is much easier to swim along the bottom than to fight surface waves. Remember to save enough air to return to shore along the bottom. If an empty tank forces you to swim on the surface through large waves, be sure all your equipment is strapped on securely.

Diving from Boats: Operate a safe diving boat. Stow tanks so they do not roll, and don't overload (remember divers have lots of heavy equipment). Have a ladder for getting in and out of the water easily.

Beware of squalls and fog. If heavy fog is a possibility, stay in the immediate vicinity of the boat.

Proficiency in seamanship increases safety and pleasure. A diver who knows how to choose accurate bearings, for example, will be able to return to a spot with ease. For accuracy, select well-defined objects that are far apart and that line up or superimpose. Two sets are needed, preferably on lines that intersect at 90 degrees. With good bearings you can anchor within 10 feet of a chosen point, a mile or so from shore.

When operating a boat around submerged divers, keep completely clear of the area of bubbles. Currents can carry bubbles some distance from their point of origin before they break the surface, and a swimming man is usually well ahead of his surface bubbles. The diver, for his part, should ascend vertically if possible and surface cautiously, listening for any boat that may be in the vicinity.

Diving boat should have a ladder or platform. Boat at right has both. Platform is light, easily detachable.

HOW TO CHOOSE BEARINGS

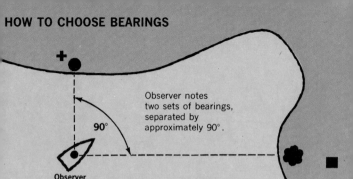

Observer notes two sets of bearings, separated by approximately 90°.

90°

Observer

POOR BEARING

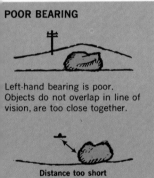

Left-hand bearing is poor. Objects do not overlap in line of vision, are too close together.

Distance too short

GOOD BEARING

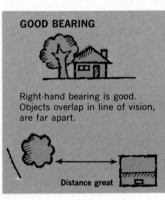

Right-hand bearing is good. Objects overlap in line of vision, are far apart.

Distance great

First Dives: Start as you did in the pool. Choose a shallow spot about chest deep, and practice clearing the mask and hoses, removing mouthpiece, and sharing air. Proceed out to water just over your head, go through these procedures again, and try ditching and recovering equipment. A partner should hold the jettisoned gear to prevent loss in case you don't retrieve it all on the first try. You will be surprised to find how much harder these basic operations are when attempted in a lake or ocean. But as you become accustomed to the changed environment, the old mastery of movement and equipment achieved in pool training will return.

Sensing Direction: Which way am I supposed to go? How do I return once I get there? Sense of direction is easily lost underwater because of reduced visibility. Think about the problem before starting down. Note the following: sun's position, direction of the current, direction of wave surge, and direction of the anchor line, if any. If a compass is used, note position of the needle with respect to the shore line or some other prominent feature. On the bottom, perceive the orientation clues present in the environment.

Bending kelp (top) is orientation clue.
Ripple marks on bottom are generally in line
with wave crests. Sea fans (right)
stand at right angles to prevailing currents.

Navigation: Most people cannot swim in a straight line without training. The ability to do so is useful and comes with practice. Pay constant attention to orientation clues such as those pictured on pages 62–63.

It is often necessary to measure distance. Counting fin kicks can be satisfactory if the swim is done at a constant speed. For this the diver should learn the rate at which he covers distance by calibrating himself over a known course. Measurement by arm lengths is surprisingly accurate, if one wants to pause or alter swimming speed. Use only one arm. While swimming, extend arm ahead, place fingers lightly on bottom and leave them fixed there as you pass over. Let arm move back until in line with the body, then reextend and repeat. Each arm length measures 6 to 8 feet.

Search: The novice may think systematic searching methods belong only to highly specialized and advanced diving. They don't. A diver constantly finds himself only a short distance from a goal yet out of visual contact, so that a

SEARCH PATTERNS

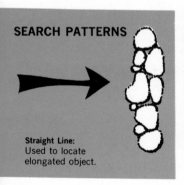

Straight Line:
Used to locate
elongated object.

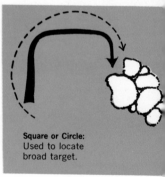

Square or Circle:
Used to locate
broad target.

search is necessary. Since random wandering can waste precious bottom time, knowledge of searching techniques is very important. An efficient search establishes a pattern that systematically eliminates one place after another, examining each area only once, and leaving no territory uninspected. The pattern to use depends on objectives, terrain, and variable factors such as water clarity.

To find a canyon, elongated reef, or other linear feature, swim a straight line perpendicular to the objective. A square or circle pattern is efficient for finding a broad reef or rock pile of large dimensions. Grid patterns are useful for smaller objects such as a wreck, coral head, or lost piece of equipment. Employ a spiral grid when the probability of finding a small object is greater at the point of origin of the search (when a tool is dropped off an anchored boat, for example). If the exact location is completely unknown, use a zigzag pattern. Spacing between adjacent lines of the pattern is determined by underwater visibility. Swim just

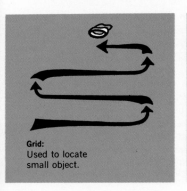

Grid:
Used to locate
small object.

Spiral Grid:
Used to locate small
object in immediate vicinity.

close enough to your previous track so the zone you are inspecting barely overlaps the path just surveyed.

Buoyancy Adjustments: Even experts can misjudge proper buoyancy. Rather than returning to shore to doff or don weights, try the following. When underweight, pick up a stone or other heavy object. When overweight, use your air supply to partially inflate a plastic bag, collecting bottle, or life jacket. Be sure to bleed air from these when ascending or you'll shoot up too rapidly. Seek help from your partner if compensation is too difficult.

For typical weight requirements, see the table on page 33. Add four to eight pounds for stability in strong waves or currents in shallow water.

You should have extra flotation gear in reserve. For instance, you may have to compensate for a fresh tank that has a different buoyancy than the one you are replacing.

Failure to correct buoyancy can ruin a dive. You'll have to work harder, breathe harder, use air faster, come up sooner.

Buddy System: Cooperation with a partner reduces hazards and increases capabilities enormously. It must be realized, however, that the buddy system has its limitations. Do not take unnecessary risks just because a partner is present. Know your partner's limitations. Do not, for example, exhaust him if he is a slower swimmer. Maintain visual communication or, in turbid water, hold a short rope (buddyline) or a harness strap between you, or hold hands. If you lose track of each other, stop to search. Create noise by banging a metal object on your tank and rise a few feet from the bottom (where the water is generally clearer) to look for bubbles. If these methods fail, surface and watch for bubbles.

Top: Improvise to correct buoyancy.
If overweight, bleed air into plastic bag; if
underweight, carry stones. Buddy-line
(above) prevents separation in turbid water.

Underwater Communication: Divers can communicate with each other by writing on slates, by hand signals, and by sound, although speech is ineffective beyond a few feet. Jerks on a buddy-line can serve as signals. A hand motion of slitting the throat universally means "terminate the dive." Any carefully prearranged set of signals can be used. For the system of signals that is standard in military diving, see the *Navy Diving Manual* available from the U.S. Government Printing Office, Washington, D.C.

Ending the Dive: The time to terminate is while you still have a good reserve of strength. You'll need energy to swim back to shore or to your boat, plus a little extra to

Four commonly used
underwater signals: (1) All OK;
(2) Ear squeeze; (3) Wait;
(4) Out of air, or Terminate dive.

cope with the unexpected. If your return path is at all hazardous (surf, currents, rocks, entangling plants, etc.), end the dive well before air is exhausted. Then, if you must, you can make an underwater pass through the difficult area. Be sure your partner understands clearly that you are terminating.

Diving in the Dark: Darkness, which might be encountered at night, in caves, or in turbid water, presents special problems in orientation and navigation. Divers who can expect any of these situations should be prepared with lights, guidelines, and buddy-lines.

Once a diver becomes quite skilled, he can attempt a 69

night dive (perhaps to observe a nocturnal creature). If so, he should know precisely what to expect as to waves, currents, turbidity, etc., in order to offset the reduction of efficiency caused by darkness. The diving boat should display a light to guide return.

Diving Below 30 Feet: Once you feel comfortable at 30 feet, descending farther is relatively simple, though the need for caution increases. Foam suits compress, reducing their insulation capabilities, ascents take longer and require decompression, and the air supply is used sooner. Nitrogen narcosis and cold water can lessen coordination, and mental and physical tasks become harder. In some respects, however, deep diving is easier than shallow. Wave surge decreases, temperature is less variable, and, in spite of reduced illumination, you can see farther because the water is clearer. A capable, athletic beginner should log at least eight hours of ocean time underwater before going deeper than 30 feet. (Eight hours underwater will require about twelve to twenty dives.) Divers who are less adept should proceed more slowly.

Emergency Ascents: This technique is needed infrequently, but is worth knowing, if only for psychological comfort. If one stays calm and acts efficiently, consciousness is retained for at least two minutes without drawing a breath. You have this period to regain the surface in an emergency, if you do not consume precious oxygen in panic and useless exertion.

Exhale as deeply as possible (to prevent air embolism), inflate your life vest or other flotation gear, jettison the weightbelt, and continue exhaling forcefully as you ascend. Emergency ascents can be made safely at rates of up to 5 feet per second.

A strong guideline should
be used in every exploration of a
cave or tunnel. It's
easy to get lost without one.

underwater environment

5

As divers become adapted to the underwater they usually turn to activities of some sort to sustain and stimulate their interest in the new environment. These may be purely recreational, or they may involve study of the underwater world—such aspects as the topography and composition of the bottom, character of the water, currents, waves, biological organisms present, etc.

But the underwater, like the land, combines areas that are dull with those that are fascinating, and it may take some investigation on your part to find interesting diving spots. You can get tips from local divers and fishermen, from maps, magazines, and books. A study of aerial photographs may show submerged reefs, seaweed beds, unusual wave patterns, or other features worth exploring. Also, if you fly to a vacation spot, take a good look at the coast as you pass over it.

Camera-toting diver met
this curious rockfish in undersea
area of varied marine
life and interesting topography.

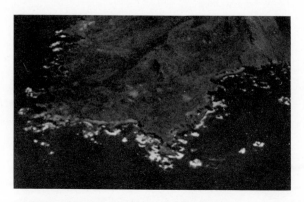

BOTTOM COMPOSITION AND TOPOGRAPHY

In general, hard bottoms (rock, coral) support denser populations of plants and animals than soft bottoms (sand, mud). If you are looking for some fish for dinner, something interesting to photograph, or just for exotic scenery, you are more likely to achieve your goal if you dive among rocks.

Remember, however, that many organisms are highly selective in their preference for substrate. If you are out to collect a particular species or observe a certain community, be sure you know beforehand what type of bottom it inhabits. Lobster, for example, are rare over mud, but an eelgrass community thrives on such a bottom.

The topography of the environment—its features of relief or unevenness—is usually important. Expect a flat terrain to be more sparsely populated than terrain with ledges, caves, crevices, or cliffs. This is because an uneven environment provides much more available surface for sedentary organisms, it furnishes hiding places for small animals

74

Offshore islets and scalloped
shoreline (top) indicate bottom
where biology probably will be
abundant, like that on opposite page.

and for juveniles of large species, and it provides dark places for nocturnal creatures to inhabit in daytime. When waves or currents are present, the resulting turbulence attracts feeders by dispersing nutrients. Many organisms are choosy about the relief features as well as the composition of their surroundings, so be sure you inquire about the preferences of a specific creature before seeking it.

An important factor contributing to diversity of life, known as "edge effect," occurs where two different types of environment join each other. Such an area often is especially rich in numbers of species, because the organisms which prefer one type of environment mingle with those preferring the other at the edges or junction of the two.

75

ROCKY ENVIRONMENTS

Rock bottoms may be continuous hard surfaces, or they may be composed of individual stones, or of a combination—individual stones scattered over flat sheets of rock. Bottoms consisting predominately of individual stones are subdivided into pebble, cobble, and boulder bottoms. Pebble bottoms are covered with small stones up to 1 or 2 inches across, and are usually the remains of beaches. Cobbles are larger stones, up to 9 to 12 inches in diameter, and typically occur on river bottoms or offshore from present or former rivers. Boulders are larger than cobbles and are common where rocky cliffs or hillsides erode into immediately adjacent streams, lakes, or coastal waters.

Continuous rocky bottoms can be subdivided into pavement rock (predominately flat surface with little relief),

Two types of rock bottoms:
(top) boulder-strewn, and (opposite)
broken rock grading into
pavement bottom at base of cliff.

ledges (vertical faces up to 4 feet high, often overhanging and horizontally elongate), cliffs (elongate, vertical faces more than 4 feet high), irregular (vertical relief up to 4 feet, but, unlike ledges, not horizontally elongate), and pinnacles (vertical projections higher than 4 feet, not horizontally elongate).

Avoid pebble and cobble bottoms in swift currents or in shallow water where there are large waves. Strong water movement tends to move these smaller stones about vigorously. This crushes and grinds up any living organisms present, so that such areas are relatively barren. In calm water or below the level of intense wave surge (usually 20 feet or deeper), pebble and cobble environments can be very heavily populated because they offer large surface areas as well as many crevices for hiding. Usually the communities of organisms populating the upper surfaces of individual stones are entirely different from those occupying the lower surfaces. Plants, for example, are common on the tops of rocks; encrusting animals such as sponges, bryozoans, and attached mollusks prefer the underside.

The same generalization holds for communities of the continuous rocky surfaces. Quite different groups inhabit vertical versus horizontal surfaces, the undersides of overhangs versus the tops, or the peaks of pinnacles versus the bases. This great diversity makes these environments interesting places to study or photograph, and to hunt food and adventure.

SEDIMENTARY ENVIRONMENTS

Sediment is any congregation of hard particles ranging from fine mud, through very coarse sand, to small pebbles. It is created by the erosion of the continents as streams and rivers carry off waters resulting from rain- and snowfall. At times of heavy precipitation, large quantities of sediment are deposited at the bottoms of lakes and coastal waters. When there is turbulence in the overlying water due to rapid stream flow or large, storm-generated waves, much of the sediment comes into suspension and is transported away by currents. Aquatic plants or animals dwelling in the turbulent area may lose their protective surroundings and perish unless they burrow deeper or extend their attachment downward.

A current will deposit a heavy sediment load when calm water is reached or when the waves die down as a storm abates. Organisms in this area will be buried unless they can escape by excavating or growing upward rapidly. Most

78

Sediment bottom is often rich in burrowing forms of life. Diver here is digging to catch rapidly burrowing animal.

of the sediments of streams, rivers, and coastal ocean water are subjected to this intermittent suspension, transport, and deposit.

A few animal species are adapted for survival in such unstable sediment environments. These include mollusks, worms, burrowing anemones, sand dollars, and some vegetation with deeply penetrating roots. The richest communities, however, tend to become established where water movement is sufficient to prevent stagnation but not strong enough to bring the sediments into suspension frequently. Look for good diving areas in quiet lakes or bays, or where islands, coves, or rocky headlands provide protection from wave surge. However, if turbulence is present, it will reduce visibility by bringing sediments into suspension.

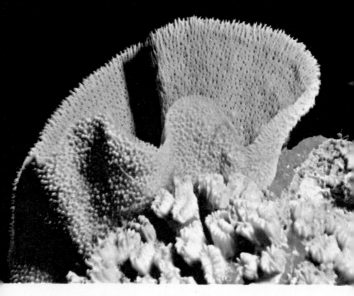

CORAL REEFS

These large stony formations are produced by tiny polyps. They are perhaps the most beautiful of underwater environments, teeming with fascinating biology. Often the structures incorporate other shell-building creatures—mollusks, protozoans, and certain plants. And the various species of corals are themselves quite remarkable.

Massive coral reefs are found only in tropical climates, and are a strong lure for vacationing divers. A *fringing* reef occurs near the shore on the submarine shelf of a land mass. A *barrier* reef develops farther out, perhaps at the margin of the continental shelf, and is usually richer in biology than a fringing reef. *Atolls* are reefs enclosing a lagoon; no land mass is present. All material above the high-water mark has been cast up from the reef itself.

BEDS OF VEGETATION

Aquatic plants enrich an environment by providing food for grazing animals, surfaces for clinging or crawling animals, and crevices for concealment from enemies.

Underwater plants attach to rocks or grow on sedimentary bottom in quiet waters. They range in size from thin brown films, like scum on the sand, to great submarine "trees," the giant kelps, over 200 feet long. Most aquatic plants are flexible and bend easily so that a diver can usually slip through thick plant growth, provided he is careful to avoid entanglement.

The longer aquatic plants usually grow toward the surface, where the upper portions float together, forming a canopy. Examples are found among the underwater grasses, the West Coast kelps, and the sargassum weeds.

81

Opposite: One of the many
beautiful organisms found in coral
reef. Above: Sargassum weed
forest shelters variety of small animals.

SUBMARINE CANYONS

All the continents are surrounded by broad, relatively flat terraces called continental shelves, created by the erosive action of the waves striking the edges of the land masses. At the outer borders of the shelves are the continental slopes, where the bottom suddenly becomes much steeper and drops down to the floor of the deep sea. The shelves are slashed in many places by deep trenches, or submarine canyons, that disgorge onto the continental slopes.

The heads of the submarine canyons (the ends nearer

Above: River of sand spills
down head of underwater canyon.
Top right: Diver studies
sea life on canyon cliff.

the shore) are sometimes close to shore and in shallow water. Here is diving at its finest. The canyon walls fall off abruptly, so that shallow water lies immediately adjacent to water of considerable depth. As a result, it is possible to observe deep-water organisms in quite shallow locations, not only strong swimmers such as fishes and squid, but also sluggish animals like starfish, nudibranchs, and worms. Even deep-water sessile (non-moving) creatures, seaweeds, and attached invertebrates such as sea fans, may occur along the rim of the canyon, probably produced

83

by spores or larvae brought up by currents from below.

A steep-walled canyon may have a "turbidity current," created when sediments traveling parallel to the shoreline are diverted into a seaward flow through the trench. In your explorations, avoid those areas in submarine canyons where sediments settle; concentrate instead on the rocky slopes and cliffs where long-lived communities develop. As a beginner, do not yield to the temptation to wander downward into canyons. You may soon be in depths beyond your capabilities.

CAVES AND TUNNELS

In entering small caves or any place where obstructions impede direct passage to the surface, carefully anticipate such problems as orientation and possible entanglement. If the cave is too large to be illuminated by light from the entrance, a guideline and compass are necessary. Remember that the interior surfaces of caves are usually covered with fine sediment which is easily stirred. Once in suspension it can block your view of the entrance.

If a large or tortuous cavern is to be explored, carry spare equipment, including extra lights and Scuba. A small tank with a lightweight single-hose regulator can be strapped to the regular Scuba. Have a Seevue gauge for reading tank pressures. A calm, capable partner is essential, and a third diver standing by is good insurance.

WRECKS

Wrecks offer much of the biological interest common to caves. They can also yield souvenirs and salvage. Maps are available that show accurately the locations of many wrecks. Sunken ships deteriorate at different rates, depending on

their structure, exposure to heavy seas, and the type of encrusting, drilling, or boring organisms present. Some ships
are torn apart in months while others may be preserved
for centuries.

Enter wrecks with caution. Jagged edges are common,
and Scuba bubbles accumulating in a compartment can
cause sections to shift or collapse. In hunting for objects,
concentrate as much on the area around the wreck as on
the ship itself.

85

Wrecks yield souvenirs,
salvage, and animal life. Divers above
collect biological specimens
from drive shaft of wrecked freighter.

WATER SCIENCE

Bottom topography is only one of the factors that make for interesting diving. Equally important is the nature of the overlying water. This includes such factors as temperature, visibility, currents, wave surge, and water-borne nutrients. Following are some basic facts about these phenomena. (To help the diver learn even more, there are excellent books on the subjects of *oceanography*, or saltwater science, and *limnology*, or freshwater science. See Bibliography, page 158.)

Dissolved Nutrients: Water that is nutrient-poor will not support luxuriant communities, no matter how favorable other circumstances may be. Conversely, when water is nutrient-rich it can support communities even when other conditions are adverse.

As organisms feed, they incorporate nutrients into living tissue. The death and decomposition of these organisms supplies nutrients for succeeding generations. Since dead organisms usually sink and decompose on or near the bottom, the important minerals they contain tend to accumulate in deeper waters. Therefore, any physical processes that bring these nutrients up into shallow areas will tend to encourage biological development there. Two such processes are upwelling and mixing by waves and wind.

Upwelling: When wind blows water away from the shoreline (a wind-generated current), deep water upwells to replace it, thereby keeping the sea level constant. This upward movement of water is large-scale and fairly continual.

A wind-generated current does not move in the direction of the wind. In the northern hemisphere, the flow at the surface is at a 45-degree angle to the right (clockwise on the compass) of the wind. Thus, ideal conditions for up-

UPWELLING

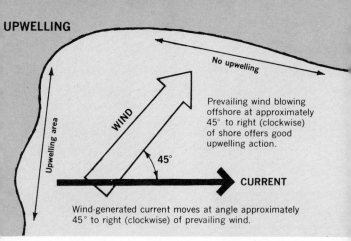

No upwelling

Upwelling area

WIND

45°

CURRENT

Prevailing wind blowing offshore at approximately 45° to right (clockwise) of shore offers good upwelling action.

Wind-generated current moves at angle approximately 45° to right (clockwise) of prevailing wind.

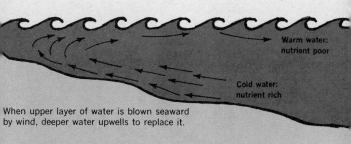

Warm water: nutrient poor

Cold water: nutrient rich

When upper layer of water is blown seaward by wind, deeper water upwells to replace it.

welling will occur when the wind flows offshore at an angle 45 degrees to the right (again, clockwise) of the coastline, thereby generating a current that flows directly (i.e., at a 90-degree angle) away from the shore.

In the United States, the prevailing winds tend to blow

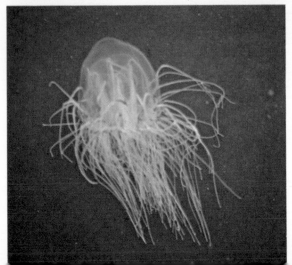

from the northeast, the north, and the northwest. To allow upwelling from such winds, a shore must be oriented so that water lies westerly to southerly from it. Lakes, bays, and coves, for example, will probably experience most upwelling along their northern and eastern shores. In the case of islands and headlands, upwelling can be expected on the southwestern sides.

Mixing: In moderately deep water, wind and waves cause mixing, a haphazard flow or turbulence made up of countless small currents and eddies. Turbulence increases with the size and spacing of the waves and the shallowness of the water.

Mixing keeps the water full of oxygen and distributes food particles, so that areas where it is intense are apt to be full of things to see or photograph. Be careful, however, of extreme turbulence, which can cut down visibility, toss you about roughly, and separate you from your equipment.

Currents: These range from small, meandering flows to huge, well-charted "rivers" (such as the Gulf Stream) that usually occur well offshore. Currents transport upwelled nutrients to new locations and disperse food particles, eggs, larvae, and other suspended organisms. They also enrich many island environments, pinnacles, and fringing coral reefs.

The large current systems of the oceans determine the character of thousands of miles of coastline. The Gulf Stream, for example, carries tropical water from the Caribbean Sea northward along the Atlantic seaboard. On the west coast of the United States, the California Current transports cold water southward from the Gulf of Alaska, thereby fostering cold and temperate communities. At the same latitude there are tropical coral reefs in the Atlantic and temperate kelp beds in the Pacific.

89

Top: School of planktonic
shrimp form dense layer near bottom.
Left: Small jellyfish
is transported by currents.

DANGEROUS ORGANISMS

In searching for good diving spots, remember to be wary of harmful underwater creatures, both plants and animals. Animals, though rarely aggressive, must be respected. It is the passively dangerous organisms that are most troublesome to divers.

Entangling Plants: Kelps and marine grasses can tie up Scuba apparatus, or even arms and legs. They are tough and slippery, and it is important not to exhaust yourself fighting them. Extricate yourself (or your partner) calmly and methodically. If you don't have a knife, you can break kelp by nicking it with a fingernail and bending.

Use the same caution with wires, ropes, lines. Always carry a knife or cutters when working near them.

Dangers to divers: (from left) spines of squirrel fish; entangling kelp; moray eel; urchin spines and sponge spicules.

Cutting and Puncturing Animals: Coral, mussels, and barnacles can cut and scrape skin or rubber suits. Be careful not to let underwater currents brush you against rough surfaces. Sea urchin spines puncture skin. They crumble easily, so use care in removing them.

Dangerous but Usually Nonaggressive Animals: This category includes the moray eel, grouper, black sea bass, and many others that may be harmless in one area but easily provoked to aggression in another. If you plan to hunt such animals for food or sport, be sure to inquire about the temperament of the local species before setting out after them. Certain rays and eels can generate harmful electrical charges. Keep on the lookout for them—and give them a wide berth.

Venomous Animals: These inject a toxic substance or venom through a puncture, bite, or cut inflicted on their victim. Since they rarely are aggressive, injury usually results from careless handling or unintentional contact. Common species include scorpion fishes and sculpins, sting rays, skates, catfish, octopus and squid, jellyfish, certain anemones, stinging corals, and some long-spined sea urchins. Venoms usually are intensely painful and sometimes require medical attention. Hot water containing Epsom salts usually alleviates the pain. Wounds should be cleaned in warm water to remove slime, mucus, or tissues of venomous animals.

Poisonous Animals: These are creatures whose flesh is toxic when eaten, a fact to be remembered by divers who like to eat the rewards of an underwater hunt. There is no sure rule for judging edibility, since a species may be edible in one location and poisonous in another. Oysters, mussels, clams, and certain fishes may become poisonous through feeding on the microscopic algae that occasionally appear in such quantities as to color the water. So check local sources before eating any unfamiliar marine food.

1

2   3   4

Divers beware: venomous
squid (1); electric ray (2); spines
of sculpin (3); flesh of puffer
fish which may be poisonous (4).

ACTIVELY DANGEROUS ANIMALS

These are more fearsome and spectacular, but can be avoided by the exercise of normal caution.

Sharks: Of the more than 250 known species of shark, only about a dozen ever have attacked man, and these infrequently. Statistically, sharks are a minor menace to divers compared to such hazards as fatigue. Nevertheless, the presence of a large shark in a diving area is something a diver must be prepared to deal with. Most important is to keep calm. Avoid jerky, excited movements, rapid swimming kicks, or waving arms. Move slowly, with determination, and keep facing the animal as you retreat. Swimming on the surface may excite a shark into action. Instead, swim submerged to your boat, or back to shore.

Blood or juices from a wounded fish may excite a shark. Carry speared fishes on a very long stringer and remove them from the water promptly. If a shark attacks your catch, let him have it. Stay clear of water that might contain blood; you may pick up the odor.

Barracuda: The solitary Atlantic barracuda, most common in the waters off Florida, can grow to 8 feet long. A voracious feeder, it has a large, sharp-toothed jaw, and it sometimes attacks swimmers. The schooling variety, Pacific Coast, does not. Proceed as with shark.

Killer Whales: A large animal which may grow to a length of 30 feet, the killer whale is a rapacious feeder. He has made no recorded attacks on divers, but he feeds on seals and could easily dispose of a man. Dives should be terminated or canceled if killer whales are known to be present.

Seals and Sea Lions: Ordinarily, these are curious and even playful creatures. They have been known to attack, however, so they should not be provoked.

94

Atlantic barracuda (bottom) and sand shark (with remora, middle) have attacked swimmers. Killer whale (top) has not, but avoid it.

95

collecting

The diver who collects specimens of underwater life has fun and becomes a keen underwater observer. Want to try it? Here are some pointers.

If you are a beginning diver, seek slow-moving or attached organisms such as corals, starfish, seaweeds, or shelled creatures. Those lightning-quick minnows take plenty of skill to trap. If you want things as ornaments or souvenirs, there are beautiful corals and shells for the gathering. More ambitious collectors preserve seaweed and soft-bodied animals, projects that require some expense for materials. Small quantities of bottles, mounting paper, preservative, etc. are inexpensive, but a large collection can cost $20 or more to mount. You can also collect animals that preserve well by drying. Don't be in a hurry to build a collection. With experience you will become more selective about the specimens you choose to add to it.

Attached animals, such
as this colorful sea anemone, and
slow-moving animals
are usually easiest to collect.

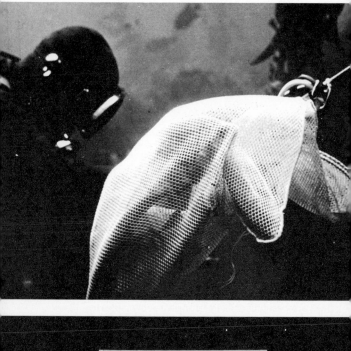

Net bag to carry specimens
(top) allows necessary water flow;
slurp gun (bottom) sucks
in small, rapidly moving animals.

GATHERING SPECIMENS

The first step in collecting is to find the specimens—not so easy since many animals hide or camouflage themselves. Sea fans (gorgonian corals), sponges, large shells, and seaweeds are not hard to spot. To dislodge attached organisms you may need a scraper, knife, or even a crowbar and hammer.

Be careful in collecting and carrying specimens to keep them as much in their natural state as possible. Delicate shells and soft-bodied animals can be carried in bottles (fill the bottle with water *before* descending, so it won't implode).

Sometimes you will encounter a desirable creature but not have the equipment to get it. Improvise. An urchin spine, handled gently, makes an excellent needle for fishing tiny things from crevices. Clam shells held closed between the fingers can substitute for a carrying bottle, as can an empty snail shell. A mussel shell makes an excellent scraper, and crushed invertebrates in a bottle may lure small fishes to entrapment if you forget a net or a slurp gun (a sucking device for capturing small, rapidly moving animals).

On a long dive take a sack to accommodate your gear and specimens. Plastic bags can be tucked in the cuff of your rubber suit and are good for seaweeds, but punch small holes in them to let water escape. Use nets for slow-moving or dangerous animals. Many sand-dwellers burrow rapidly; for this quarry have a shovel, trowel, or other digging tool at hand. Large fish are usually speared or stunned with a bang stick, a device that explodes blank cartridges. Have stand-by flotation gear in case your specimens should weigh you down at the end of the dive.

PRESERVING, LABELING, AND IDENTIFYING

Don't let organisms deteriorate after taking them from their habitat. Either keep them in water for the trip home or carry them in a bottle of preservative.

Fleshy specimens, such as fishes, large seaweeds, and soft-bodied invertebrates, must be kept in preservative. Shelled specimens kept in preservative will retain their soft, fleshy parts intact. To preserve the shell alone, dissolve the soft parts by gentle immersion—no longer than thirty minutes—in a heated solution of sodium bicarbonate or other alkali. Organisms with very little fleshy tissue (corals, small seaweeds, starfish, etc.) can be dried.

To dry thin and delicate specimens such as seaweeds, spread them on a backing of mounting paper and press between blotters for several days. (A strip of cheesecloth between plant and blotter prevents sticking.)

Specimens can often be stored in their preserving fluids. Shells, skeletal structures, and large dried specimens may require cabinets or protective boxes if they are delicate or have long spines or projections. A specimen mounted on paper or cardboard can be displayed under glass like a picture, or stored in a flat position, while pressed plants can usually be stacked atop each other safely. Store dried specimens in dry places.

Some aquatic organisms require a combination of preserving techniques. Preserving followed by drying, for example, is useful for large, fleshy starfish.

Many transparent or translucent organisms can be beautifully preserved in plastic. The liquid plastic, as well as casting and polishing equipment, is available at hobby stores and biological supply houses. The process is as follows. Preserve organisms in alcohol, changing the fluid several

100

Top: Seaweeds are protected and attractively displayed in plastic mount.
Right: Collector arranges seaweed specimens on immersed mounting paper.

times to remove water from the specimen, then immerse for a day or two in an organic liquid such as xylene. After the xylene has replaced the alcohol, the specimen can be immersed in the liquid plastic. Because the plastic is soluble in xylene, it is free to permeate the tissues before hardening, thereby preserving their transparency. But be sure that water and alcohol are completely removed first, or opacity will result.

Label the specimens in your collection properly. Note the name of the specimen, date, time, place, and depth of collection, collector's name, and any remarks.

Identifying uncommon organisms is often difficult. If friends, diving clubs, hobby organizations, or the local library and museum fail to provide the answer, contact a professional biologist, giving him all pertinent data, and, if possible, a specimen that he may keep.

THE HOME AQUARIUM

Maintaining an aquarium, an enjoyable pastime in itself, can also yield valuable, otherwise unattainable information about the behavior, habits, and requirements of organisms.

Do not overload an aquarium. It is a restricted system and there must be enough water to assimilate all the waste products of the inhabitants. Active creatures, such as fishes, generally require more water than sluggish or attached organisms such as snails, anemones, and plants. A gallon of water will usually be adequate for a fish one inch long. Five gallons will support five such fish or one larger fish perhaps 6 inches long. Aerating the water or circulating it through a charcoal filter doubles the load a given volume of water can carry.

Because the close quarters of an aquarium facilitate

Special care must be taken when handling and preserving a delicate organism, such as this tube anemone.

transmission of infectious diseases, plants and animals should be inspected daily and removed to a separate tank or discarded if sickness develops. Keep a supply of water in reserve so that the aquarium can be completely flushed if murkiness or turbidity appears. Cloudy water usually results from a rapid increase in suspended microörganisms —primarily bacteria and protozoa—and indicates that the tank is overloaded or something is dead and should be removed.

Try to simulate conditions of the natural environment in your aquarium. The proper temperature, light conditions, food, or associated creatures may be vital to the survival of a particular organism. It may even be necessary to use water from the actual spot where you found your specimens.

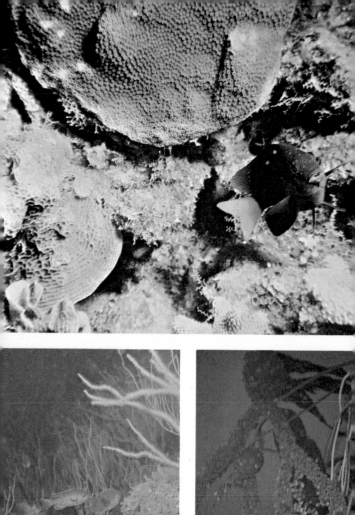

STUDYING COMMUNITIES

You may have found a particularly fascinating underwater cliff or a small reef or submarine meadow teeming with life. This is a place you would like to know more about, but you seem to have reached the limit of understanding to be achieved by casual observation. If this is the case, try studying it as a community. You will need several week-ends, at least, to gather and assemble the different scraps of information about the inhabitants of the place and their ways of life and, in the process, your fascinating spot will become positively captivating. Such a project is actually quite similar to the kind of work that is done by marine biologists. And, like the scientists, you should proceed scientifically.

A community is a natural association of plants and animals whose lives are interdependent. A community study finds out what creatures are present and what their relationships are. Usually it is food that links them all together, but other, more subtle, influences, such as shelter from enemies or from harsh physical conditions, can be equally important.

Collecting and Identifying: The first step is to find out what is present. Don't spend hours trying to identify a few difficult creatures. Call them species A, B, C, etc. It is very important that you collect and preserve a typical specimen of each of these unknowns and label it with its special designation. Later a species may disappear, or you may find you are calling two different species by one name, and will need to refer to your original designation. Don't omit something just because it is small or infrequent. Sometimes organisms which appear minor turn out to be the ones that control or direct the entire community.

There may be many small animals hiding in the vegeta- 105

Top: Small coral-reef microcosm. Far left: Community in which blacksmith fish eat small attached animals that feed on microscopic plankton. Left: Kelp blades host microcommunity.

tion. Enclose some of these plants in plastic bags; work quickly to keep the organisms from escaping. At home, put the plants in an aquarium or dish with two or three crushed moth balls and swirl the water vigorously. Chemicals in the moth balls will anesthetize the tiny animals and they will settle to the bottom, facilitating collection. Make lists of all plants and animals collected. As your study proceeds, the lists will grow.

In fact, from the beginning you should record in a notebook all observations of relationships among the different species. Make a note when you see one creature eating another, or using it for protection, or as a place to roost or hide, or even when the association has no obvious purpose. Include a date and time of day for every observation. Gradually, links between community members become apparent.

Mapping: When you have listed most of the creatures present you can start mapping the community. Such a map needn't be a precise representation of the bottom. It should depict roughly those features of the topography that seem important to the community—cliffs, current and wave directions, crevices, overhangs, composition of the bottom, and any significant changes therein. It will probably be necessary to prepare both vertical and horizontal cross sections. Sketch in the locations of the various species by shading or with different colors. Include a date for which the community map is representative. You will probably find that some species change location with time. Active swimmers, such as fishes, at times may range widely throughout the community although tending to prefer certain spots over others. These locations should be indicated and notes added as to over-all range.

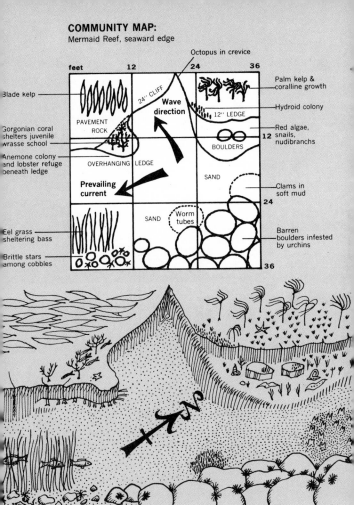

COMMUNITY MAP:
Mermaid Reef, seaward edge

Octopus in crevice

feet   12   24   36

24" CLIFF

Wave direction

Blade kelp

PAVEMENT ROCK

12" LEDGE

Palm kelp & coralline growth

Hydroid colony

Gorgonian coral shelters juvenile wrasse school

Red algae, snails, nudibranchs

BOULDERS

12

Anemone colony and lobster refuge beneath ledge

OVERHANGING LEDGE

Prevailing current

SAND

Clams in soft mud

24

Eel grass sheltering bass

Brittle stars among cobbles

SAND

Worm tubes

Barren boulders infested by urchins

36

Relationships: Once the community map is fairly complete, attention can be focused on identifying relationships between the organisms. You will soon note that various levels or hierarchies exist within a given category of relationships. As an example, take the category of food. The basic level here is the plants. Plants, of course, do not eat anything. They manufacture their body substance from water, dissolved minerals, and sunshine, but they are eaten by the lowest hierarchy of animals, the herbivores (plant eaters). The lower carnivores (meat eaters) comprise the next level and these in turn are eaten by one or more hierarchies of higher carnivores.

You may find in your community a group of animals which are never seen taking in any kind of food. Often these animals are attached to the bottom and remain in one place (mussels, worms, barnacles, oysters). These "filter feed" on microscopic particles suspended in the water (diatoms, dinoflagellates, bacteria, nonliving particles, etc.). Other animals become uneasy and do not feed when divers are present. Still others may feed only at night. If you cannot determine a creature's diet by direct observation it may be necessary to anesthetize the specimen (again with crushed mothballs) and examine the stomach contents by dissection.

You may want to chart the relationships you discover between feeders and their food sources. Interconnecting lines indicate relationships. When carnivores eat several species the chart becomes quite complex and is called a food web. The chart may show that there are two or three groups of species which have few or no interconnections. This usually indicates the presence of more than one community. Thus your field of inquiry is enlarged. 109

Top: In feeding experiment
shy moray eel is coaxed from lair.
Left: Sponge provides
shelter for fragile sea spider.

Time and Communities: Study the daily and seasonal time changes in a community in the same way described above for analyzing food relationships. As your observations accumulate, correlations will appear between the environmental information and community activities.

Some communities are stable and persist for years, such as kelp beds and coral reefs. Others are transitory and may last for only a few weeks, like animals that encrust on a seaweed blade. Some communities—plankton, for example—are suspended in the water and move great distances each day with the currents.

Light and dark can cause important changes in communities. Species that are enemies can inhabit the same location if one is nocturnal and the other diurnal. Many animals, such as fishes, move to new areas at night for feeding or other purposes. Oftentimes, creatures that dwell in dark caves or crevices by day (lobster, abalone) will be

found moving in the open at night. Use of waterproof lights at night will disrupt normal activities somewhat, but a great deal will be unchanged or can be deduced from what is seen.

Certain interesting changes are timed according to monthly tidal cycles. Grunion, for instance, spawn when the moon is full. Other animals, such as vast schools of deep-water squid, may spawn over sandy bottoms on a yearly basis. In spawning season, animals may exhibit very changed habits of feeding and behavior, sometimes becoming quite tame and easy to handle. Underwater vegetation, too, displays seasonal characteristics which influence the dependent communities.

Not much knowledge of time changes in underwater communities has been accumulated, so your own time study, if conducted carefully, could be of considerable scientific value.

Successive communities on buoy (from left): at one month, crustose algae; at 3 months, coralline algae; at 6 months, moss animal.
Above: Daytime haunt of nocturnal spiny lobsters.

STUDYING A SINGLE SPECIES

As your knowledge of underwater creatures increases, you may decide to do a concentrated investigation of a single interesting species. Several approaches to this are possible. An active and intelligent animal, such as a fish, may display interesting behavior. A slow-moving animal with a less-developed nervous system may be limited to a few simple and obvious responses, yet have a natural history that is fascinating. Perhaps the way it captures food, protects itself from enemies, survives harsh physical conditions (storms or unusually high or low temperatures), or relates to certain other species, will prove intriguing.

Life Cycles: It can be fascinating and often challenging to work out the life cycle of some particular species. Many aquatic plants and animals change so greatly between juvenile and adult stages that biologists have sometimes classified individuals in the two stages as two different species.

A good way to begin is to collect smaller and larger specimens of the creature and arrange them in a series according to size. If the organism changes markedly with growth, this series may give you clues as to what the younger or older stages may look like. This method is useful if the changes are gradual, but when an abrupt metamorphosis occurs the transition stage may be difficult to find. Sometimes the juvenile organisms can be raised in an aquarium until the transition stage is observed. If the juvenile stage is unknown, an adult male and female can be maintained in an aquarium in hopes of obtaining offspring. If the adults can be watched closely in nature during spawning season, it may be possible to gather fertilized eggs or larvae at the proper time. Some adults will spawn

Markings of juvenile angel
fish (left) and adult angel fish (right)
are so different they could
be mistaken for different species.

or release eggs and sperm if kept out of water a few minutes. To obtain young, mix a batch of eggs with a drop of sperm in a cup of water, and then transfer to a small aquarium after about half an hour. Embryonic or larval development may require from several days to a few weeks. Every few days, collect several of the larvae and preserve them in vials, so that you will have a developmental series. Note their environmental preferences. If they are planktonic (suspended in the water), you can guess where to seek them in nature.

Organisms frequently inhabit quite different environments during their various life stages. Your search will be taxing but never dull.

113

Sergeant-major fish guards eggs
laid on rock (1); blacksmith is drawn by
noise of generator (2); wrasse
seeks parasites on angel fish fin (3).

ANIMAL BEHAVIOR

Observation of animal behavior is a particularly challenging pursuit, since the appearance of a human in an underwater microcosm usually disrupts the normal behavior of the more intelligent inhabitants. The diver may have to make repeated visits before he is taken for granted. And he may have to use oxygen rebreathers and other special techniques to lessen disturbance. (The rebreathers are, of course, for experts only.)

Spawning, nest building, protection of the young, and courtship rituals can be spellbinding activities to watch. They may be very complex and require long periods of observation. Many animals—for example, fishes like the garibaldi and stickleback—build special nests or other structures prior to the actual spawning period. Sometimes even a special plant is cultured to provide a suitable home for the eggs. Other creatures, such as squid, salmon, or grunion, require less elaborate preparations. Huge numbers may suddenly appear and spawn, then die or disappear.

Cleaning behavior is a phase of underwater activity which was brought to the attention of scientists by amateurs. Many small fish and crustaceans feed by removing parasites from large fish. Some cleaners are so meticulous in their operations that they actually enter the mouth and gills of the large fish. Instances are known of large fish coming considerable distances to the dwelling site of a particular cleaner.

Much of our knowledge of aquatic animals is derived from observations made in waist-deep water. There is much more to be done at greater depths, gathering information about deep-water movement patterns, migrations, attack and escape behavior, feeding, etc.

ANIMAL ASSOCIATIONS

A curious fact is that extremely dissimilar animals are sometimes close associates—for instance, pilot fish and large sharks, and starfish and oysters. When an association does not seem to exist for the obvious reasons of food provision or protection, considerable sleuthing may be needed to discover its causes.

Record all the information you can gather about the animals in an association, both from your own observations or from reading. Note whether the association occurs in young or in old animals, or only at some particular stage in their lives. What are the feeding habits? Does one animal eat the leftovers from the other's meal? How close is the association? If it is very intimate, one animal may be protecting the other, perhaps in return for a service fur-

116

Animal associations (from left):
Worms inhabiting grooves of starfish;
shrimp in convolutions of
abalone; remora riding on whale's jaw.

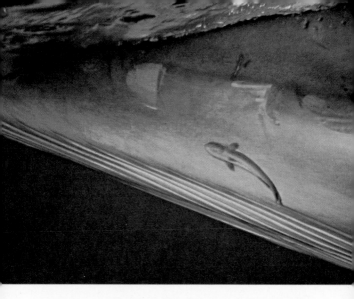

nished by the sheltered species. Or one may be a parasite.

An association is often quite mysterious. Some tiny fishes, for example, find shelter among the tentacles of certain tropical anemones, which sting other creatures viciously; yet the associating fishes are immune. How and why is this environment safe for them?

In another association, occurring between starfish and certain small worms, the worms are known to detect and follow the scent of the specific starfish. From how far can a worm detect the scent of its host? Would another species of starfish be attractive in the absence of the usual host?

Associations sometimes are helpful in finding or collecting animals. An inconspicuous species that associates with a larger, more obvious host, can often be obtained by seeking the host.

117

ENVIRONMENT AND DISTRIBUTION

Science is finding out more and more about the environmental conditions preferred by certain organisms. It is often amazing how closely the distribution of various plants and animals correlates with the existence of a particular environment. The rocky rims of submarine canyons, for example, may have species that occur there, and sparsely or not at all elsewhere. Sometimes a more common environment, such as an underwater cliff, pinnacle, or cave, supports a specialized assemblage of organisms. We may not know in some cases why certain organisms prefer a given en-

vironment; we know only that they occur there. Yet this fact alone can be built on. It provides suppositions as to where a certain species may be found, why it is not more abundant in other regions, how it can be maintained in the laboratory.

Amateur divers often have opportunities to visit areas where scientists have not yet studied conditions. If you find familiar organisms extending into new environments, or unusual locations supporting creatures you do not recognize, it may be of value to collect and record what you see. You will, in any case, add to your understanding of the underwater and increase the interest and enjoyment of diving.

119

Offshore pinnacles often
display unusual species, such as the
California hydrocoral (left).
Top: Divers examine brink of canyon.

recovery

7

Possibly the most adventurous activity in diving is recovery of valuable objects, both man-made and natural, from the bottom of the sea. There are fossil beds, shipwrecks, and sunken civilizations still waiting to yield up their treasures. It's useful, if you plan to explore an important site, to notify interested scientists and historians. Your findings may be of value to them, and they, in turn, can supply information about recovered objects.

Recognizing man-made objects underwater is not as simple as you may expect. Wave surge usually breaks up the structures of old wrecks, while rust, encrusting animals, and seaweed complete the disguise.

Reefs are the likeliest places to search for wrecks. Look for straight lines or sharp angles in the encrusted rubble that is usually a feature of reefs. A pile of rounded cobbles in deep water may be the ballast of a decomposed ship

Diver escorts his find
to surface. Recovery of valuable
objects is one of
diving's most exciting activities.

(since cobbles occur naturally in surf zones only). Cannon, anchors, and shafts have elongated shapes that catch the eye. Sometimes, in searching a smooth mud or sand bottom, a fathometer will reveal the irregular contours of a protruding object. A metal-detector is another useful tool for locating completely encrusted artifacts.

RECOVERY TECHNIQUES

The first step in actual recovery is to mark your position. A small buoy will do until you can install a permanent surface buoy. In an area of heavy boat traffic, or where curiosity seekers are a problem, it may be more practical to mark your location by means of bearings. If the objects you seek are scattered over the bottom, map the area carefully by charting underwater landmarks.

Heavy objects often can be raised with surprising ease by the use of air, which has a lifting power underwater of

roughly 60 pounds per cubic foot. Depending on the requirements, containers of different sorts can be used to hold the buoyant air—plastic bags, barracks bags, buckets, 55-gallon drums. Flexible containers are prone to leak and are most suitable for brief, simple operations. Air is supplied from a compressor or by bleeding a standard Scuba tank.

Winches may be necessary once the object is brought to the surface; if air is not used for underwater lifting, a winch is handy for this phase also. Tidal winches can be improvised. At low tide, attach a buoyant floating object, like a 55-gallon drum, to the underwater object by a taut rope. When high tide raises the object, tow it shoreward till it runs aground. At next tide, repeat the process, and so on.

Hydraulic methods may be necessary for uncovering and digging. Near shore, it may be possible to jet with a garden hose attached to the regular water main. At sea a simple ½-inch water pump does a good job.

The air-lift device, powered by compressed air, sucks up mud and stones, and is handy for recovery of small objects buried in sediments.

123

Left: Lifting-bag is inflated with air from tank. Above: One diver releases small marker buoy, another airlifts sand from around buried object.

124

Crucifix and semiprecious
stones (top) were recovered from Spanish
wreck. Above, fossilized
mastodon teeth from Florida riverbed.

FOSSILS

Caves, ledges, cliffs, and shelves that were exposed when sea levels were lower and that were subsequently covered with sediment are proving to be rich sources of remains of early man and animals. Fossils of extinct creatures such as mastodons and giant sloths have been found in Florida caves and streams, while a subterranean spring near Venice, Florida, has yielded parts of more than two hundred human skeletons.

Living fossils—creatures previously known only from fossil deposits—have been discovered in the sea. Examples are a wavy top-snail discovered on the isolated Sacramento Reef in Mexico, and a primitive mollusk (Neopilina), dredged off South America, which has contributed enormously to the understanding of evolution in the animal kingdom.

ANTIQUITIES

Some of the most thrilling underwater recoveries are objects from ancient sunken ships or submerged cities and villages. The Atlantic and Caribbean are dotted with wrecks dating from the days of the Spanish Main to recent times. The Pacific Coast occasionally yields a treasure dating to the Spaniards, but most of its material is from Indian cultures that flourished on the beaches. The Mediterranean has given up priceless Roman and Greek antiquities.

Some of the better-known recovery operations include that of a Roman argosy at Mahdia on the Mediterranean by Jacques Yves Cousteau, salvage of the Spanish galleon El Capitán off the Florida Keys by Navy Lt. Harry Rieseberg, and study of sunken Port Royal in Jamaica by explorer-inventor Edwin Link.

TREASURE SHIPS

Although at least fifteen hundred ships carrying gold coins, bullion, silver, or gems have been recorded as lost or sunk in the oceans, a host of difficulties prevents recovery of this submerged wealth.

Extensive research is usually necessary to discover the age, approximate location, and actual cargo of a treasure ship, and to ascertain if its cargo has not already been salvaged. Recovery may be hampered by depth or surf conditions, burial in mud or sand, and by the size of the ship itself. Searching for a treasure in a wrecked ship is much like looking for the scattered contents of a box in a collapsed four-story building, with the added difficulty of working underwater. Any valuable cargo which may be brought

Above: Ancient jars recovered from Mediterranean by team of Jacques Yves Cousteau. Opposite: Professional diver inspects fittings on boat hull.

to the surface is then subject to claims by both the descendants and government of the original owners of the ship. Finally, the diver may expect to find himself in competition with treasure-hunting professionals, usually corporations that are able to finance well-organized and scientifically equipped operations.

Diving for lost treasure is always adventurous, whether treasure is found or not. At the same time, there are many sure ways of deriving financial rewards from diving, even if you miss out on the adventure. Amateur divers can hire themselves out to perform a variety of underwater tasks that includes recovering lost gear, cleaning and inspecting boat bottoms, and taking photographs. Charge reasonable fees and you will be in demand.

photography

The aspiring underwater photographer should understand basic photographic principles before he attempts to film the submarine world. To get satisfactory results in this strange environment, he will have to adjust his technique to the underwater's many complexities of light, motion, clarity, etc. The light-ray effects of refraction, reflection, and scattering are especially troublesome.

Refraction: Bending of light rays when they pass from air into water or from water into air is called refraction. This causes an increase in the focal lengths of lenses, so that the angle of coverage is slightly reduced. Visually, refraction causes objects to appear about a third closer than their actual distance. Since the camera sees what the diver sees, focus is not influenced, but when using flash, remember not to underestimate the distance which will be illuminated, since the object is farther away than it appears.

Now where did he go?
Colorful, exotic subjects await
the diving photographer;
special techniques yield fine shots.

Annoying light patches may appear on the bottom in shallow water. These are caused by the lens action of large wave crests, which focuses the refracted light rays into areas of brightness and shadow.

Reflection: Loss of light by reflection at the surface depends primarily on the height of the sun. For flat, calm water, 2 percent of the solar radiation is lost when the sun is directly overhead. This increases to 35 percent loss when the sun is 10 degrees above the horizon. Photograph as close to midday as possible, when the light is maximal.

Scattering: Particles suspended in water scatter light rays. This affects photographs by degrading image quality severely, making them hazy or foggy. Where sharp definition is essential, camera-to-object distance must be closely watched. Avoid shooting objects at farther than one-fourth the distance you can see (some critical photographers reduce this to one-fifth or less). Farther away, objects will be hazy, although still useful as background.

Lens Openings for Underwater Photography if Surface Light-Meter is Used						
Depth (in feet)	Limit of underwater visibility (in feet)					
	10'	15'	20'	25'	30'	40'
10'	3x	2x	1x	1x	1x	—
15'	4x	3x	2x	1x	1x	1x
20'	5x	3x	2x	2x	1x	1x
25'	6x	4x	4x	2x	2x	1x
30'	—	5x	4x	3x	2x	2x
35'	—	6x	5x	4x	3x	2x
40'	—	6x	5x	4x	3x	3x
45'	—	—	6x	5x	4x	3x

To read: (1) Locate depth at which picture will be taken; (2) estimate and locate on table the limit of underwater visibility; (3) where related lines intersect, read number of additional stops to open lens. Also estimate amount of light being lost due to surface reflection (see diagram page 131) and open lens an additional 1½ to 2½ stops, as required.

REFRACTION

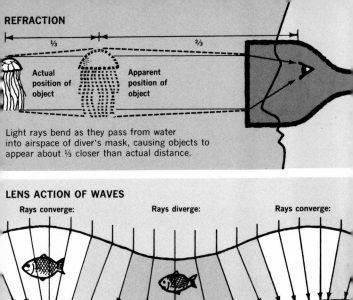

Actual position of object

Apparent position of object

Light rays bend as they pass from water into airspace of diver's mask, causing objects to appear about ⅓ closer than actual distance.

LENS ACTION OF WAVES

Rays converge: **Rays diverge:**   **Rays converge:**

Bright spot   **Shadow**   **Bright spot**

LIGHT LOSS BY REFLECTION

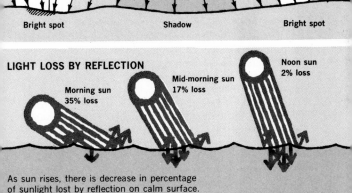

Noon sun 2% loss

Mid-morning sun 17% loss

Morning sun 35% loss

As sun rises, there is decrease in percentage of sunlight lost by reflection on calm surface.

1

Color: Water does not absorb colors uniformly. Red is most strongly absorbed, followed by orange, yellow, blue, and finally green. Suspended particles and plankton can change this order somewhat, so that the predominant color at the depth where you are working may vary from blue to yellow. Usually, only blue or green light is present in significant amounts below 20 to 25 feet, so color correction by filters beyond this depth is futile.

Lighting: If you have an underwater light-meter, exposures are determined as on land for depths down to 30 feet.

You can work with a surface light-meter, too, by housing it in something like a watertight jar. It can be used as a point of departure for determining f-stop, though variable underwater conditions make it less than completely depend-

132

Plankton has filtered out blue
light, leaving green cast at bottom (1).
Garibaldi at 10 feet (2) is
orange, at 50 feet (3) dull yellow.

able. To compensate for initial light loss at the surface, the diaphragm must be opened one and a half to two and a half stops beyond the surface reading, depending upon the height of the sun. Additional light loss occurs with increasing depth and decreasing visibility, and larger diaphragm openings are required, as shown on the table on page 130. Thus, if the sun is high in the sky, the diaphragm must be opened one and a half stops initially. If you are working at a depth of 10 feet and visibility is 20 feet, one additional stop opening is required, or a total of two and a half stops beyond the surface light-meter reading.

Flash contributes little illumination at distances greater than 10 to 15 feet because light is readily absorbed and scattered underwater. In turbid waters, flash is apt to de- 133 grade picture quality because of back-scattering. Particles suspended in the water reflect light from the flash unit, and this washes out large sections of the picture.

For distances up to 10 feet, #5 flash bulbs are generally most effective; #22 bulbs are best up to 15 feet, but they may collapse below 30 feet. Both blue and white tinted bulbs give good color rendition with daylight film.

EQUIPMENT

The general principle for diving activities—keep your gear simple and to a minimum—is particularly important for underwater photography. And all gear should be relatively shock resistant. Small size and streamlined contours are highly desirable, as considerable energy is necessary to transport a heavy, bulky camera, while sharp corners can cut or puncture the photographer's diving suit.

If only one control is available on your camera, it is better to have an adjustable f-stop than an adjustable focus. If no adjustments can be made, a very fast lens with good depth of field gives best results. Calibrations must be highly legible.

A wide variety of watertight camera housings is available in plastic, wood, and metal. All should be tested at the depth at which they will be used before placing equipment in them. Lower the housing on a line from the surface, so that you won't get hurt if a structural weakness should lead to an implosion. A promising development is the 35mm camera developed by Nikon that is waterproof and pressure-proof to a depth of 160 feet.

Keep lenses clean. Dust and dirt which might not prevent you from getting good pictures topside can spoil underwater shots. Take care to prevent damage to your camera

Double flash (top) gives more light. Left: Spot on film is caused by particles reflecting flash. Above: Camera in plexiglass housing.

equipment from corrosion and water leakage.

Flash units must be taken apart and rinsed after exposure to salt water. Give special attention to plugs; it may be necessary to polish male and female surfaces with emery cloth after they dry. Test-fire your flash unit before reloading the camera, using a flashlight bulb which allows repeated tests.

Still Cameras: Lenses have to be fast, since openings of f3.5 or wider are constantly required. And, because of the refraction and image-degradation problems noted earlier, wide-angle lenses are preferred. A sportfinder for viewing quick action is extremely useful, and a camera that takes several pictures rapidly is handy to have when fast-moving animals appear. Because of the impossibility of reloading underwater you should use 35mm film with 36 rather than 20 exposures.

Movie Cameras: Underwater movies also require a wide-angle lens, preferably one with a focal length of 13mm or less. (The 25mm lens normally used for topside movie work is good underwater only for close-ups.) Since settings and adjustments are not easily made underwater, a lens with great depth of field is an asset.

Movies also require considerably larger diaphragm openings than still pictures. With a fast film, an f-stop of 2 will permit work to a depth of 30 feet in ordinary water; an f-stop of 1.0 will work to 60 feet.

Many underwater photographers get good results with the smaller 8mm cameras; they are easy to handle and inexpensive to operate. Of course, 16mm film projects a larger image and its 24-frames-per-second speed is usually ideal. Whatever you choose, be sure your camera has a long film-run per winding.

Tripod (top) guarantees stability.
Diver (far left) focuses on
coral with watertight 35mm Nikonos.
Left: Rolleimarine twin lens reflex.

FILMING TECHNIQUES

Let's consider stills first. For color work, Hi-Speed Ektachrome film is recommended. However, while you are learn-
ing the special problems of underwater photography, it is
less expensive to work with black-and-white film such as
Plus X or Tri X (with Accufine development).

Select small, clearly defined subjects. With moving objects, head-on views are least likely to be blurred. To at-
tract fish to your shooting area, crush a sea urchin or
other delectable invertebrate. As you work, be careful not
to stir up bottom sediments. Hold the camera steady, even
if you have to add extra weights for stability. Exhale and
shoot.

If you pan with a fast-moving subject, you can expose
longer, thus compensating somewhat for poor lighting.
Since underwater lighting is flat and continuous, attention
must be paid to creating contrast. Shoot from angles pro-
ducing silhouettes, or frame objects against contrasting
backgrounds. Use films and filters which improve contrast.
The familiar technique of underexpose and overdevelop is
often useful.

138

Varied backgrounds and unusual
properties of underwater light (above
and right) can enhance and
dramatize underwater photographs.

Movie technique also has its tricks. A fast film, such as Professional Ektachrome, is most satisfactory. Brace yourself well before shooting; add extra weight if necessary. You can learn to control the body roll that results from fluttering your flippers. If the shooting situation is unstable, try increasing film speed to thirty-two or even sixty-four frames per second, light permitting, to slow the action down.

It's good to hold the camera on an underwater subject longer than is usual in land filming; audiences need additional time to recognize unfamiliar aquatic life.

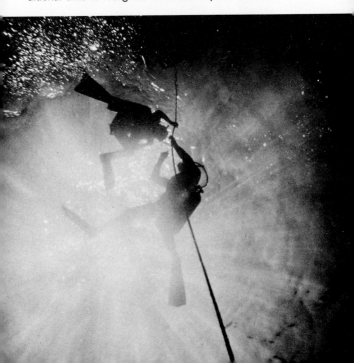

hunting
&
spearing

The underwater teems with creatures that are both good eating and good sport. In United States waters the diver can go after many species of fishes, as well as clams, oysters, scallops, shrimp, abalone, crabs, lobster, octopus, and squid. Make sure that any hunting you do is in compliance with local fishing regulations. And be careful, too, not to get in the way of commercial fishermen and rod-and-reel sportsmen. If you are hunting for sport, with no specific prey in mind, go to places that have a reputation for good fishing. Fishing activity on the surface probably means good hunting below.

Equipment: In clear water and for short distance pursuits, it is keener sport to dive with snorkel only. However, searching for prey in turbid water or at depths greater than 20 feet is best done with Scuba, particularly if the hunter is a novice.

141

Sierra fish (left), native to
Gulf of California,
gave underwater fisherman
long, scrappy fight.

From top: Hand-thrown five-tine spear; Hawaiian sling powered by rubber band; arbalete with trigger release. Wear Scuba when hunting deeper than 20 feet.

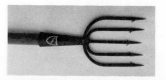

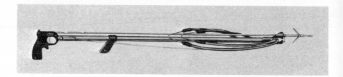

There is a bewildering assortment of gear designed for spearing, prying, and digging, but the beginner is wise to seek modest-sized prey with simple equipment. Simple spears, such as the five-tine and the Hawaiian sling, are best for small fishes (up to 24 inches long). The five-tine should be used for soft-fleshed bottom fish, such as flounder. The sling is powered by an elastic band which is held in a stretched position and released when striking. Avoid using slings when visibility is low; no line is attached to the shaft, and you may lose it if you miss a shot. For maximum effectiveness, keep spears sharp.

142   For larger animals, the more complex spearguns—arbaletes

—should be used. They are powered by two or more bands and fire more smoothly and accurately. The spear may be attached to the gun by 15 to 20 feet of line, so that it isn't necessary to get as close to the prey as with a single-band sling. For large prey, powerful heads are available which drive the point forward with great force.

Breakaway flotation devices can be used with most spear-guns instead of a line. When the spear is discharged, this gear detaches from the gun and is towed by the prey until the animal tires and can be landed.

Stalking: As a rule, fish are most abundant in water where the bottom is irregular or where it drops sharply from a shallow to a greater depth. In the latter environment, larger deep-water fish will be found preying on the shallow-water animals.

Safety

Handle spearguns with extreme care, especially when entering and leaving the water and when reloading. Never point the spear at your own or anyone else's body. Be absolutely sure of the identity of your target. Under murky conditions, shorten the line between spear and gun, so that the spear cannot penetrate beyond the range of visibility. Always load and fire calmly.

Top: Diver's arbalete has
break-away attachment. Above: Fine
broadside shot (left)
and well-camouflaged flounder.

You can often discover the hangouts of a particular quarry by inquiring at the local diving or fishing store. Know what its preferences are for food, environment, and shelter. Nocturnal animals, for instance, spend the day in caves, crevices, or under rocks.

Camouflage is a common defense. The appearance of your animal in nature may be quite different from what you see in a fish market, aquarium, or book. Flat fishes are often lightly covered with sand, so look for protruding eyes and gills. Rockfishes, sculpin, and scorpion fish lie quietly in seaweed of matching color. Constantly scan the water around and above you; there are many desirable mid-water fishes, such as barracuda, amberjack, and yellowtail, that often slip by unobserved.

Spearing: The first rule of spearing is not to scare fishes with jerky movements or splashing of the surface. Frequently a fish will hesitate for a look just after you encounter him. This is the hunter's golden moment. Try for a broadside shot from within 6 feet. Never attempt spearing a fish at an angle greater than 45 degrees, since the fish's scales may deflect the spearhead.

Some fishes won't confront the diver, but will follow close behind, so whirl about from time to time and be ready to shoot. Other species keep their distance if you are at their level, but are less cautious if you are above or below them.

Some tricks: Hold your breath during the approach; bubbles can frighten shy animals. Fishes may abandon caution when food is present, so try attracting your prey with a broken sea urchin or an injured small fish. If a fish swims behind an obstacle, approach by an indirect route, since he will probably be watching for your appearance by the most direct route.

Use gloves to catch spiny lobsters and seize them force-fully. They can swim backward rapidly, so don't leave any exits open when you grab for them in a crevice.

With abalone, it is important to break the animal's suc-tion grip on the substrate suddenly and without warning. Otherwise it can cling so tightly that the shell is torn loose, leaving the body attached to the rock.

Handling Your Catch: An injured, struggling animal can be hazardous. Even small fishes may have sharp spines or other protuberances that cut and puncture. Some species carry painful venoms in the spines (sculpin, scorpion fish, rays). Larger animals can bite, slap, butt into, or exhaust their captors. Hold your prey away from your body by the spear shaft, and wait until it is thoroughly exhausted be-fore removing it from the water. Then, holding it by the gills, pull it with you headfirst as you ascend. If the fish is small, remove the shaft and run a line (stringer) through the gills to tow it by. Don't tow any fish in water where there are sharks or other dangerous animals that may be attracted by blood. Instead place the catch inside a water-proof bag. On reaching your boat, give the shaft or stringer to your partner or tie it to a cleat. Haul yourself aboard be-fore pulling up your prize.

It's easy to rig a floating container for catch. Wrap a rope around an inner tube to provide hand grips, and fasten a net, sack, or small washtub to the rope at the inner peri-meter of the tube.

Remember to avoid exhausting yourself when handling a catch. Many a fine prize has been abandoned or has fought loose because the spearfisherman forgot his own limits. Don't become so loaded with lobster or abalone that you can't swim back to the surface.

Top: Swimmer handles exhausted
black sea bass by gills. Above: Stringer
through mouth and gills
allows catch to be towed easily.

careers in diving

10

Many young men find sport diving so stimulating that they decide on careers as professional divers. They soon find out that professional work is far different from recreational diving. Challenge gives way to routine, and jobs must often be done under grueling environmental conditions. On the other hand, professional divers are usually well paid for enduring the hazards and discomforts of underwater operations. This is definitely a profession for young men, but not for anyone who expects to lead an easy, adventurous life Scuba diving for pay.

Professional divers are, in fact, in ever greater demand. Science, industry, the military, and law enforcement agencies increasingly depend on skilled divers to perform many essential tasks. These will certainly multiply as man becomes more proficient at working underwater and exploiting the resources of the sea.

Diver repairs windows
in large aquarium. Professional
divers are in ever greater
demand, but work is strenuous.

Industrial and Community Work: Divers serve industry in a variety of ways, for example in the building, inspecting, and repairing of tunnels, bridges, and harbor facilities. They do underwater surveys for oil companies before offshore drilling is attempted. Television and the movies also need divers to work in underwater filming.

Communities, too, are making use of diving skills, particularly in police work such as search and recovery. Many forces have their own specially trained Scuba units.

Scientific and Military Needs: Universities and government agencies send oceanographers underwater to collect samples and measure such localized phenomena as currents, water layers, and submarine illumination. Divers also observe the dynamic processes of the oceans, such as erosion, upwelling, and changes in the sea level.

Military diving—operations of defense as well as salvage

At work underwater: Diving geologist (above, left) and construction worker. Navy frogmen (opposite) will inspect submarine's hull.

and repair—is usually done by naval personnel, the "frog-men," as they are called.

Biological Products: Divers are contributing much to our knowledge of world fishery resources by gathering information on the behavior, distribution, and ecology of commercially important animals.

Diving to harvest plants and animals is not usually profitable unless the organisms collected are quite valuable. In many countries divers gather creatures such as sponges, pearl-bearing oysters, precious coral and shells, and red algae which is processed into agar for use in biology and medicine. Profit from all these operations is too small to permit them on a large scale in the United States, where divers' pay is higher. An exception is abalone, which are plentiful enough on the Pacific Coast to support a fishery there in the gathering of these large mollusks.

151

man's future underwater

11

Man has finally begun to open the underwater frontier. He is now at home in the shallow depths—thanks to Scuba—and the future holds no limits for exploration or for utilization of underwater resources. Techniques will certainly be developed to reach the enormous mineral and oil deposits in the sea floor; already, oil in the continental shelves is being tapped by ingenious drilling methods. There are vast supplies of energy in the waves, tides, and currents. The magnitude of the food riches in the oceans can only be guessed at. Meanwhile, scientists are speculating about future human communities living in submerged, self-sustaining environments.

The work of the immediate future will be in charting the shelves and islands, studying their geology and biology, and describing the layers of the deep sea. Perhaps your own observations will contribute to this knowledge.

U.S. Navy's bathyscaphe,
Trieste, made record descent—
35,800 feet—into
Mariana Trench in Pacific.

TECHNOLOGY

Technology is constantly improving the tools needed in underwater research. A basic requirement for progress is a substance suitable for use in submerged apparatus. It must be able to withstand erosion, abrasion, great pressures, and unfavorable biological action. As yet, such a material has not been found.

Scuba itself is far from perfected. Wastage of gas in present-day systems is high. Because air is 21 percent oxygen, and each exhaled breath is still rich in this element, being perhaps 14 percent oxygen, 90 percent of Scuba's gas supply is unused. A Scuba that utilizes 100 percent of its gas supply and can be used with safety by the general public will be a development of prime importance, allowing

Crew of oceanographic expedition (left) triple-check equipment before each major cruise. U.S. Navy aquanaut (below) leaves Sealab experimental chamber.

the pace of exploration to be greatly stepped-up.

At present, underwater man must obey rather shallow depth restrictions. With elaborate preparations and modified apparatus, depths below 200 feet can be safely reached and useful work done. But such operations are costly and quite beyond the means of the average individual or even the majority of diving organizations. The physiology of man under pressures greater than 10 atmospheres still demands much investigation. But there is reason to believe that man can become more nearly a marine animal. Technology may provide communication capabilities matching those of whales and porpoise. We may even learn to imitate the marine mammals that dive to great depths regularly and with no apparent difficulty.

CONTROL OF THE DEEP SEA

The deep sea is a realm which only a handful of men have ever seen. What we know of it is learned chiefly from instruments and from haphazardly gathered samples. Its creatures are usually recovered dead or dying, often mangled beyond recognition.

Efforts to penetrate the awesome depths of the deep sea are continuing, however. As land space and land resources are consumed, efficient use of the oceans will be imperative. They contain twice the space of all the world's dry land combined and, as is increasingly evidenced, sizable concentrations of valuable minerals as well. Getting at these resources will be enormously difficult since a large proportion of them lies 12,000 feet or more below the surface.

Deep-sea submersibles, free from surface connections, are now in existence and others are being developed. The Piccard bathyscaphe has descended 7 miles to the bottom of the deepest known trench. Cousteau's *soucoupe sousmarine,* designed to go down 3,000 feet, is small, saucer-shaped, highly maneuverable. Startling physiological advances are being recorded by the navies of several countries, as well as private individuals using special mixtures of breathing gas. Penetration of the world's oceans, now in its initial stages, promises to be one of the most exciting human achievements of the twentieth century.

ORGANIZATIONS

The individual may wonder how he or she can participate more fully in underwater activities. Diving clubs—there are several hundred in the United States—offer distinct advantages to members. They simplify the problem of finding a diving partner and serve as clearing houses for local news

Midget submarine *Alvin,*
an exploring vessel designed
to withstand great
pressures of ocean depths.

and information about advanced techniques and equipment. Group members contribute to the purchase of expensive items—compressors, cameras, special rigs, even boats—which are usually beyond the means of individuals. Instruction for beginners is offered, and nearly always there are experienced divers to help you learn a new technique or go a little deeper.

Individual clubs often join to form councils or other high-level organizations. These serve to help define aquatic policy locally, at the state level, and nationally, so that the interests of divers are taken into consideration.

bibliography

BASIC AND ADVANCED TECHNIQUE

Complete Illustrated Guide to Snorkel and Deep Diving, by O. Lee. Doubleday & Co., 1963.
130 Feet Down: Handbook for Hydronauts, by H. & S. Frey. Harcourt, Brace, Inc., 1961.
The New Science of Skin and Scuba Diving, Conference for National Cooperation in Aquatics. Association Press, 1962.
U.S. Navy Diving Manual. Navships 250-538, Government Printing Office, Washington, D.C. 20025.
U.S. Navy Salvage Manual. Navships 250-000-9452, Government Printing Office, Washington, D.C. 20025.

MARINE SCIENCES AND IDENTIFICATION

American Sea Shells, by R. T. Abbott. Van Nostrand, 1954.
The Earth Beneath the Sea, by F. P. Shepard. Johns Hopkins, 1959.
How to Know the Seaweeds, by E. Y. Dawson. William C. Brown Company, 1956.
Living Fishes of the World, by E.S. Herald. Doubleday & Co., 1961.
A Manual of the Common Invertebrate Animals, by H. S. Pratt. McGraw-Hill, 1948.
This Great and Wide Sea, by R. E. Coker. Harper Brothers, 1962.

NONFICTION ADVENTURE AND INFORMATION

The Silent World, by J. Y. Cousteau. Harper Brothers, 1953.
Sunken History: the Story of Underwater Archaeology, by R. Silverberg. Chilton, 1963.
The Treasure Diver's Guide, by J. S. Potter, Jr. Doubleday & Co., 1960.
World Beneath the Sea, National Geographic Society, 1967.
World Without Sun, by J. Dugan. Harper & Row, 1965.

PERIODICALS

Geomarine Technology, 1075 National Press Building, Washington, D.C. 20004.
Oceanology International, Industrial Research Publications Co., Beverly Shores, Indiana 46301.
Skin Diver Magazine, 5959 Hollywood Boulevard, Los Angeles, California 90028.
Undersea Technology, Compass Publishing Co., Suite 1000, 1117 19th Street, Arlington, Virginia 22209.

index

159